Social Issues in Literature

Political Issues in J.K. Rowling's Harry Potter Series

Other Books in the Social Issues in Literature Series:

Class Conflict in F. Scott Fitzgerald's *The Great Gatsby*

Depression in J.D. Salinger's *The Catcher in the Rye*

Industrialism in John Steinbeck's *The Grapes of Wrath*

Issues of Class in Jane Austen's *Pride and Prejudice*

Male/Female Roles in Ernest Hemingway's *The Sun Also Rises*

Racism in *The Autobiography of Malcolm X*

Racism in Harper Lee's *To Kill a Mockingbird*

Racism in Maya Angelou's *I Know Why the Caged Bird Sings*

Suicide in Arthur Miller's *Death of a Salesman*

Women's Issues in Amy Tan's *The Joy Luck Club*

Women's Issues in Nathaniel Hawthorne's *The Scarlet Letter*

Social Issues in Literature

Political Issues in J.K. Rowling's Harry Potter Series

Dedria Bryfonski, Book Editor

GREENHAVEN PRESS
A part of Gale, Cengage Learning

Detroit • New York • San Francisco • New Haven, Conn • Waterville, Maine • London

Christine Nasso, *Publisher*
Elizabeth Des Chenes, *Managing Editor*

For more information, contact:
Greenhaven Press
27500 Drake Rd.
Farmington Hills, MI 48331-3535
Or you can visit our Internet site at gale.cengage.com

Articles in Greenhaven Press anthologies are often edited for length to meet page requirements. In addition, original titles of these works are changed to clearly present the main thesis and to explicitly indicate the author's opinion. Every effort is made to ensure that Greenhaven Press accurately reflects the original intent of the authors. Every effort has been made to trace the owners of copyrighted material.

LIBRARY OF CONGRESS CATALOGING-IN-PUBLICATION DATA

Political issues in J.K. Rowling's Harry Potter series / Dedria Bryfonski, book editor.
p. cm. -- (Social issues in literature)
Includes bibliographical references and index.
ISBN-13: 978-0-7377-4022-6 (hardcover)
ISBN-13: 978-0-7377-4023-3 (pbk.)
1. Rowling, J. K.--Criticism and interpretation--Juvenile literature. 2. Rowling, J. K.--Political and social views--Juvenile literature. 3. Potter, Harry (Fictitious character)--Juvenile literature. I. Bryfonski, Dedria.
PR6068.O93Z826 2008
823'.914--dc22

2008035600

Printed in the United States of America

2 3 4 5 6 12 11 10 09 08

ED359

Contents

Chapter 3: Contemporary Perspectives on Political Issues

Introduction

In the seventeen years and seven books since the idea for the Harry Potter series occurred to Joanne Rowling on a train from Manchester to London, her bespectacled orphan with the lightning-shaped scar would grow to maturity as he fought an epic battle against the forces of evil. Along the way, the Harry Potter books would become an international cultural as well as publishing phenomenon, selling more than 400 million copies worldwide by 2008, being translated into more than 65 languages and sold in 200 countries and territories. And the story of the author of these books would become a classic Cinderella tale, as she would go from a single mother on welfare to the first person to become a billionaire through creative writing.

The overwhelming popularity of the books has prompted many people to ask: Why are they so popular among children? In addition, many of those who have probed the Harry Potter books for deeper meaning have asked: Are they simply a good read, or is there an underlying political message that the author intended to impart to children?

In terms of the first question, J.K. Rowling has offered some insight. In an interview with Judy O'Malley about *Harry Potter and the Sorcerer's Stone* in July 1999 for *Book Links*, Rowling said:

> I think that [children gaining their own power and having some control over circumstances], in a nutshell, is why they like the book. It deals with a very common fantasy for a lot of children: I must be special. These people cannot be my parents! I think we all go through that to some extent. It's just a normal part of growing up. We all want to be different. And, however happy children are, however well looked after, children are incredibly powerless. Someone else is al-

> ways calling the shots, whether it be a parent, teacher, or older sibling. So they love the idea that you can break out of that.

New York Times reviewer Michiko Kakutani explained that "the achievement of the Potter books is . . . the creation of a richly imagined and utterly singular world, as detailed, as improbable and as mortal as our own." While this fully created imaginary world is a significant attraction, the books possess two other major assets—they are well written, and they are very funny.

J.K. Rowling has also addressed the second question, of whether there is a political message to the Harry Potter series. In an interview with Meredith Vieira on NBC's *Dateline*, Rowling described the series as "a political metaphor." She explained that while there are "quite consciously overtones of Nazi Germany, there are also associations with other situations."

And in an interview at Carnegie Hall in October 2007, Rowling answered the question, Did you use the Nazi era as a model for Voldemort's reign?

> It was conscious. . . . I think most of us, if you were asked to name a very evil regime, we would think Nazi Germany. There were parallels in the ideology. I wanted Harry to leave our world and find exactly the same problems in the wizarding world. So you have the intent to impose a hierarchy, you have bigotry, and this notion of purity, which is this great fallacy, but it crops up all over the world. People like to think themselves superior and that if they can pride themselves in nothing else they can pride themselves on perceived purity. So yeah, that follows a parallel. It wasn't really exclusively that. I think you can see in the Ministry even before it's taken over, there are parallels to regimes we all know and love. . . . The Potter books in general are a prolonged argument for tolerance, a prolonged plea for an end

> to bigotry, and I think it's one of the reasons that some people don't like the books, but I think that it's a very healthy message to pass on to younger people, that you should question authority and you should not assume that the establishment or the press tell you all of the truth.

Even without Rowling's comments, there are enough clues in her life story to indicate that she is politically aware and that her politics would generally be considered left of center. The first clue can be found in the job she took after graduating from Exeter University, working for the human-rights organization Amnesty International. She conducted research on human-rights abuses in French-speaking Africa. Her continuing support for the principles of Amnesty International can be assumed by the fact that her Web site provides a link to the organization's Web site.

A second clue can be found in the name of her first child, Jessica, named for author Jessica Mitford. Rowling read Mitford's memoir *Hons and Rebels* at an early age and declared the author her heroine. Mitford was a noted political activist and member of the Communist Party. In addition, in a 2008 interview with the Spanish newspaper *El País*, Rowling declared her "real life" hero to be Robert F. Kennedy.

The political message in the Harry Potter novels has caused some to act in Harry's name, and Rowling has welcomed these efforts. As related in the article on Rowling that ran when she was a runner-up for *Time* magazine's Person of the Year 2007:

> In addition to some 300 wizard rock bands, reams of fan fiction and countless websites, the books have inspired outfits like the Harry Potter Alliance, an online group founded by Andrew Slack, 28, a consultant in Boston, around the rallying cry "The weapon we have is love." When *Deathly Hallows* was released, the group organized house parties from Australia to South America and coast to coast in the U.S. to raise awareness of genocide in Darfur, in a kind of "What

> Would Harry Do?" campaign. The parties featured performances by such bands as the Remus Lupins and the Moaning Myrtles and a podcast by Africa experts, including Joe Wilson, a.k.a. Mr. Valerie Plame. "We can be like Dumbledore's army, who woke the world up to Voldemort's return, and wake our ministries and our world to ending the genocide in Darfur," Slack urged Harry Potter Alliance members in tones of earnest camaraderie. In the days that followed, the student antigenocide coalition STAND saw a 40% increase in sign-ups for high school chapters and a 52% increase in calls to its hotline, 1-800-GENOCIDE.

When the author of the *Time* article asked her about her feelings concerning the Harry Potter Alliance, Rowling said, "It's incredible, it's humbling, and it's uplifting to see people going out there and doing that in the name of your character." She continued, "What did my books preach against throughout? Bigotry, violence, struggles for power, no matter what. All of these things are happening in Darfur. So they really couldn't have chosen a better cause."

While there is general agreement that politics is a major theme in the Harry Potter novels, critics have many interpretations of the nuances of this theme. The essays that follow explore politics in the Harry Potter series as well as contemporary perspectives on political issues raised in the series.

Chronology

1965

Joanne Rowling is born on July 31 to Peter and Anne Rowling in Chipping Sodbury, England.

1967

Rowling's sister, Diane, is born on June 28.

1970

The Rowling family moves to Winterbourne, and Joanne becomes friendly with children with the last name of Potter. In September, Joanne begins her first day of school at St. Michael's Church of England School in Winterbourne. About this time, she writes her first short story, featuring a rabbit named Rabbit.

1974

The Rowling family moves to Tutshill, along the border of England and Wales, and Joanne attends Tutshill Church of England Primary School.

1976

Rowling attends Wyedean Comprehensive Secondary School.

1983–1987

Rowling attends Exeter University, where she studies French and classics.

1987

Rowling begins working as a secretary at Amnesty International in London.

1990

Rowling moves to Manchester with a boyfriend. On a train from Manchester to London, the idea for Harry Potter comes to her. Her mother dies later in the year, on December 30.

1991

Rowling gets a job teaching English in Portugal. She works on the first Harry Potter novel.

1992

Rowling marries Jorge Arantes, a Portuguese journalist, on October 16.

1993

Daughter Jessica is born on July 27. Later that year, Rowling and her husband separate.

1994

Rowling returns to England, traveling to Edinburgh, Scotland, to be near her sister. She applies for public assistance. About this time, Rowling is treated for depression.

1995–1996

Rowling teaches French in Edinburgh and begins working intensively on Harry Potter. *Harry Potter and the Philosopher's Stone* is accepted by the Christopher Little Literary Agency.

1996

In August, Bloomsbury agrees to publish *Harry Potter and the Philosopher's Stone.* Scholastic accepts the book for U.S. publication with an advance of some $100,000.

1997

Harry Potter and the Philosopher's Stone is published in the United Kingdom and receives the Nestlé Smarties Gold Award. Rowling receives an £8,000 grant from the Scottish Arts Council that enables her to continue to focus on her writing.

1998

The U.S. edition, *Harry Potter and the Sorcerer's Stone*, is published by Scholastic. Rowling receives the British Book Award for Children's Book of the Year for *Harry Potter and the Philosopher's Stone. Harry Potter and the Chamber of Secrets* is published in the United Kingdom.

1999

Harry Potter and the Chamber of Secrets is published in the United States. *Harry Potter and the Prisoner of Azkaban* is published.

2000

Harry Potter and the Goblet of Fire is published.

2001

Rowling publishes two works under pseudonyms: *Fantastic Beasts and Where to Find Them*, as Newt Scamander, and *Quidditch Through the Ages*, as Kennilworthy Whisp. The film adaptation of *Harry Potter and the Sorcerer's Stone* is released by Warner Bros. Rowling is awarded the Office of the Order of the British Empire by Queen Elizabeth and receives it from Prince Charles. On December 26 Rowling marries Neil Murray.

2002

The film adaptation of *Harry Potter and the Chamber of Secrets* is released by Warner Bros.

2003

Harry Potter and the Order of the Phoenix is published. Rowling gives birth to a son, David Gordon Rowling Murray, on March 24.

2004

The film adaptation of *Harry Potter and the Prisoner of Azkaban* is released by Warner Bros.

2005

Harry Potter and the Half-Blood Prince is published. The film adaptation of *Harry Potter and the Goblet of Fire* is released by Warner Bros. Rowling gives birth to a daughter, Mackenzie Jean Rowling Murray, on January 23.

2007

The final book in the Harry Potter series, *Harry Potter and the Deathly Hallows*, is published. The film adaptation of *Harry Potter and the Order of the Phoenix* is released by Warner Bros.

Social Issues in Literature

Chapter 1

The Background of J.K. Rowling

The Life of J.K. Rowling

Major Authors and Illustrators for Children and Young Adults

In this biographical essay on J.K. Rowling from the Major Authors and Illustrators for Young Adults *series, the authors give information on Rowling's early life and discuss the success of the Harry Potter franchise. They trace Rowling's desire to be a writer back to when she was five or six years old and created stories about Rabbit and Miss Bee. She continued to write through school, the authors explain, and began work on the Harry Potter story when she was twenty-six.* Harry Potter and the Sorcerer's Stone *was published to enthusiastic reviews and instantly made its author wealthy and famous. The remaining six Harry Potter novels have continued to set publishing records. The Harry Potter novels have been translated into more than thirty-five languages and, according to the authors, are truly a global publishing phenomenon.*

J. K. Rowling is the second richest woman in the United Kingdom after the queen. Not bad for a single mom who was once on welfare. The British author of novels for young people caused an overnight sensation with her first book, *Harry Potter and the Sorcerer's Stone*. . . .

Translated into a multitude of languages around the world, the Harry Potter books prove the theory of globalization better than most exports. The Chinese publishing house, People's Literature, which once issued the poems of Chairman Mao, even published a boxed set of the first three Harry Potter titles in a print run of 600,000, the largest fiction printing since the communists came to power in China in 1949. The release of the Warner Bros. movie in late 2001, *Harry Potter and the Sorcerer's Stone*, breached the last strongholds of benighted people in the world who had never heard of Harry Potter. . . .

Major Authors and Illustrators for Children and Young Adults. Detroit, MI: Gale Group, 2002. Reproduced by permission of Gale, a part of Cengage Learning.

"Rowling's books have bridged political and cultural chasms," wrote Paul Gray in *Time* magazine, "they have altered publishing industries; they have even spurred censorship moves by some religious fundamentalists." By the release of the sixth Harry Potter book, *Harry Potter and the Half-Blood Prince,* in 2004, more than 100 million copies of the books were in print.

Rowling planned to continue her Harry Potter saga for seven books, spinning a magical blend of wit and fantasy—a surreal melange of "the dark juvenile novels of Roald Dahl and C. S. Lewis," according to Carla Power, writing on the Harry Potter phenomenon in *Newsweek.* Rowling is good copy—a busy mom who wrote much of her first Harry Potter adventure while sitting in coffeehouses as her little daughter napped beside her, she presents a Cinderella story every bit as fanciful as the one she concocted in her book. Rowling herself, winner of numerous awards and now employed full-time in her life's ambition as a writer, has managed to keep a semblance of private life, changing her old one-bedroom flat in Edinburgh for a Scottish estate and various apartments, and marrying the day after Christmas in 2001. With an estimated annual income of more than $40 million, she is no longer worried about lining up for unemployment checks.

Rowling's Early Life

Born near Bristol, England, Rowling grew up with a younger sister and a distinct inclination toward story-telling. Rabbits played a large part in her early tales, for Rowling and her sister wanted a rabbit very badly. Her first story, at age five or six, involved a rabbit dubbed, quite logically, Rabbit, who got the measles and visited his friend, a giant bee named Miss Bee. As Rowling commented, "Ever since Rabbit and Miss Bee, I have wanted to be a writer, though I rarely told anyone so. I was afraid they'd tell me I didn't have a hope."

Two moves took the Rowling family eventually to the town of Tutshill, near Chepstow, in the Forest of Dean along the border of England and Wales. This brought a long-time country-living dream to fruition for Rowling's parents, both Londoners, and the nine-year-old Rowling learned to love the countryside in this new abode. She and her sister could wander unsupervised amid the fields and play along the River Wye. "The only fly in the ointment was the fact that I hated my new school," Rowling once said. It was an old-fashioned school with roll-top desks and a teacher who frightened Rowling.

From Tutshill Primary, Rowling went to Wyedean Comprehensive School. "I was quiet, freckly, short-sighted and rubbish at sports," she commented of these years. Rowling confided to Roxanne Feldman in an interview in *School Library Journal* that the character of Harry's friend Hermione is loosely based on herself at age eleven. English was her favorite subject and she created serial stories for her friends at lunchtime, tales involving heroic deeds. Contact lenses soon sorted out any feelings of inferiority in the young Rowling; writing became more of a compulsion and less of a hobby in her teenage years. Attending Exeter University, Rowling studied French, something she later found to be a big mistake. Her parents had advised her that bilingualism would lead to a successful career as a secretary. "Unfortunately I am one of the most disorganized people in the world," she related, which obviously posed a significant problem to a budding secretary.

While working at Amnesty International, Rowling discovered one thing to like about life as a secretary: she could use the computer to type up her own stories during quiet times. At age twenty-six, Rowling gave up her office job to teach English in Portugal. It was there that she began yet another story that might become a book, about a boy who is sent off to wizard school. All during the time she spent in Portugal, Rowling took notes on this story and added bits and pieces to the life of her protagonist, Harry Potter. In Portugal she also met the man who became her husband, had a daughter, and got divorced.

Back in England, she decided to settle in Edinburgh [in Scotland] and set about raising her daughter as a single mother. Accepting a job as a French teacher, she set herself a goal: to finish her novel before her teaching job began. This was no easy task with an active toddler in hand. Rowling confined her writing to her daughter's nap time, much of it spent in coffeehouses where the understanding management allowed her space for her papers. In her interview with Feldman, Rowling commented that she had no idea what sort of reception the book would get, if she was even able to get it published. "I knew how difficult it would be just to get a book published. I was a completely unknown writer. I certainly could never have expected what's happened. It's been a real shock." She was able to send off her typed manuscript to two publishers before beginning her teaching post, but it was not until several months later that the happy news arrived that her long-time intimate, Harry Potter, would appear between the covers of a book in England. And then a few months later, the American rights were bought for a stupendous price and Rowling said goodbye to teaching. . . .

Introducing Harry Potter

Harry Potter, an orphan, has led a miserable life with the Dursley family, his maternal aunt and uncle. Ever since Harry arrived unannounced at their doorstep, the Dursleys have been put out, as has their vile son, Dudley. Harry has taken up residence in a broom closet under the stairs, bullied at school and mistreated by the Dursleys. Small, skinny, and bespectacled, Harry is an unlikely hero. The only thing physically interesting about Harry is the lightning-shaped scar on his forehead.

"Harry had a thin face, knobbly knees, black hair and bright green eyes," Rowling wrote in the novel. "He wore round glasses held together with a lot of Scotch tape because of all the times Dudley had punched him in the nose." That quote goes a long way to demonstrating not only Rowling's tongue-in-cheek humor, but also her sensitivity in portraying the difficulties of being a child.

When Harry turns eleven, he receives a letter. Of course the Dursleys keep it from him, but finally another letter gets through to Harry telling him that he has been admitted to Hogwarts School of Witchcraft and Wizardry. This is the first that Harry has known about his parents being wizards, or that they were killed by the evil sorcerer, Voldemort, or that he himself is something of a legend in wizard circles for having survived Voldemort's attack, which, by the way, left the scar on his forehead. Before he knows what is happening, he is swept off by the giant Hagrid, keeper of the keys at the school, on a flying motorcycle. Thus begins what Rayma Turton in *Magpies* called "a ripping yarn" and a "school story with a twist." Instead of boring math and geography, Harry takes lessons in the History of Magic and in Charms, or Defenses against the Dark Arts. He becomes something of a star at the school athletic contest, quidditch, an aerial sort of soccer match played on broomsticks. He forms friendships with Ron and Hermione and encounters students not quite so pleasant, such as the sly Draco Malfoy. He investigates the secrets of the forbidden third floor at Hogwarts, battles evil in the form of professor Snape whom Harry fears means to steal the sorcerer's stone which promises eternal life, and discovers the secret behind his scar. In short, Harry learns to be his own person. . . .

Hogwarts is a composite of the typical English public school (which is actually private in America), yet turned on its head. Harry is lodged in Gryffindor house, rivals of another house, Slytherin; his school supplies include a message-bearing owl and a magic wand. "The light-hearted caper travels

Author J.K. Rowling, who became a household name upon publication of the Harry Potter series, signs a copy of Harry Potter and the Deathly Hallows. AP Images.

through the territory owned by the late Roald Dahl," observed a reviewer for *Horn Book*, who concluded that *Harry Potter* and the Sorcerer's Stone is a "charming and readable romp with a most sympathetic hero and filled with delightful magic details." . . . A classic tale of good versus evil, as well as a coming-of-age novel with a unique flavor, *Harry Potter and the Sorcerer's Stone* is not simply a novel about magic and wizardry. As Michael Winerip commented in the *New York Times Book Review*, "The magic in the book is not the real magic of the book." For Winerip, and countless other readers, it is the "human scale" of the novel that makes it work. "Throughout most of the book, the characters are impressively three-dimensional," Winerip noted, concluding that Rowling "had wizardry inside," achieving "something quite special" with her first novel.

Rowling's Fame Grows

Even as enthusiastic reviews were pouring in from America, Rowling's second installment of the Harry Potter saga was published in England. *Harry Potter and the Chamber of Secrets* takes up where the first novel stops. Harry returns to second term at Hogwarts in a flying car, and deals with old and new characters alike. One of these newcomers is Nearly Headless Nick, a poor creature upon whom an executioner made a messy cut; another is a ghost who inhabits the girls' bathrooms, Moaning Myrtle. Valerie Bierman, writing in *Carousel*, noted that "this plot is brilliantly scary with horrible happenings, mysterious petrifyings and a terrifying conclusion." A reviewer in *Publishers Weekly* asserted that, if possible, the story is even more inventive than *Harry Potter and the Sorcerer's Stone* and Rowling's "ability to create such an engaging, imaginative, funny and, above all, heartpoundingly suspenseful yarn is nothing short of magical."

The third installment in the Potter series, *Harry Potter and the Prisoner of Azkaban*, begins when Harry is thirteen and starting his third year at Hogwarts School for Witchcraft and Wizardry. A notorious mass murderer who is a henchman of the evil Lord Voldemort has escaped from Azkaban Prison and comes looking for Harry. Despite the danger, Harry is quite preoccupied with an upcoming match of quidditch where he plays the most important position, that of the Seeker. Perhaps therein lies part of the secret to the success of the Potter books, opined Gregory Maguire in *New York Times Book Review*: "J. K. Rowling's fantasies celebrate a boy's relish in physical prowess as well as the more bookish values of moral and intellectual accomplishment." . . .

Rowling's fame and wealth continued to surge with the release of *Harry Potter and the Goblet of Fire*, in which fourteen-year-old Harry faces his biggest challenge to date, battling evil Lord Voldemort to make friendship triumphant over discord. At Hogwarts School of Witchcraft, Harry's name is picked out of the magic Goblet of Fire to compete in the Triwizard Tournament. All the usual Rowling trademarks are in this fourth book, which was so hyped that four million copies were sold even before its publication date. Overall, skeptical critics felt that the author delivered on all the hype. . . .

In addition to the books, by 2001 the product merchandising of Harry Potter items accelerated as the release of the first in a series of full length Harry Potter feature films neared. The movie, starring Daniel Radcliffe as Harry, quickly attained the popularity of the original novel. A film version of the second novel, *Harry Potter and the Chamber of Secrets*, premiered in London on November 3, 2002. On September 11, 2003, as Rowling's Harry Potter books topped the American Library Association's list of most-challenged books for 2002, Prince Felipe of Asturias presented [the author] with Spain's Prince of Asturias Concord Prize "for having helped children of all races and cultures to discover the joy of reading." This honor carried with it a $56,000 prize and a sculpture by [the acclaimed twentieth-century Spanish artist] Joan Miro.

The Harry Potter books continued in succession, with a fifth release in the series appearing to nearly one million advance orders in 2003. Called *Harry Potter and the Order of the Phoenix*, the initial release of the U.S. hard cover edition sold five million copies in the first 24 hours, and a subsequent Scholastic edition sold two million copies in 2004. Overall, the number of Harry Potter books in print approached 100 million by the appearance of the sixth in the series, *Harry Potter and the Half-Blood Prince*, which saw publication in July 2004.

A Harry Potter web site launched on May 24, 2004, coincidental with the release of the film, *The Prisoner of Azkaban*, on June 4, 2004. The web site scored 17 million visitors in its first week. On June 5 Rowling won the Bram Stoker award for best work for young readers, for *Harry Potter and the Order of the Phoenix*. On July 12, 2004 she received an honorary doctorate from Edinburgh University in Scotland. That same month, the sixth Harry Potter book, *Harry Potter and the Half-Blood Prince*, was scheduled for publication.

With all her works translated into [more than] thirty-five languages, and the subject of myriad articles, Web pages, and even book-length biographies, J. K. Rowling has indeed spawned a major book and film industry with her modest creation. "In one sense," [Paul] Gray wrote, "the boy wizard has slipped beyond her control; he is out there, everywhere, and legions of people feel a sense of ownership. But in the most important way, Harry still belongs to her. His future is in her head, as is that of the entire fictional universe she has set in motion."

In July of 2005, *Harry Potter and the Half-Blood Prince* sold 6.9 million copies in the United States in its first 24 hours of sale, breaking [Rowling's] own record for the fastest selling novel, set two years ago with *Harry Potter and the Order of the Phoenix. Harry Potter and the Goblet of Fire*, and *Harry Potter and the Order of the Phoenix*, meanwhile, were adapted into films.

Rowling added two more awards to her list in 2006. The series won Best Book honors at the Kids' Choice Awards. In addition, Aberdeen University in Scotland presented her an honorary doctor of laws degree. . . .

In its first 24 hours of availability [in the summer of 2007], *Harry Potter and the Deathly Hallows* sold 8.3 million copies in the United States and 2.6 million copies in Britain.

Events in J.K. Rowling's Life Shaped the Harry Potter Books

Sean Smith

Tracing the life of J.K. Rowling through research and interviews, biographer Sean Smith finds that events in Rowling's personal life have had a significant impact on her work. Her mother's death profoundly affected her work, Smith contends, and her sadness at losing her mother is reflected in one of the most famous Harry Potter chapters, "The Mirror of Erised" in Harry Potter and the Philosopher's Stone *(published in the United States as* Harry Potter and the Sorcerer's Stone*). Following the breakup of her first marriage, Rowling lived for a time on public assistance. Smith writes that she experienced depression during this time and created the Dementors, who are a metaphor for depression. Smith is a former newspaper columnist for the* Daily Mirror *and* Sunday People. *He is the author of several books, including* Sophie's Kiss *and* Royal Racing.

Joanne was in a far from buoyant mood when she sat gazing at the same stretch of English countryside for forty minutes on a train back to London after a weekend of fruitless flat-hunting in Manchester. She could have thought of many things: whether she was right to leave London, how her mother was doing back in Church Cottage, how her father was coping. She could have thought of the Black Horse or the Devonshire House coffee bar and more carefree times. She thought of none of these, however, because Joanne Rowling has always been a dreamer and, as she gazed out of the carriage window at some equally forlorn-looking black and white Friesian cows, she thought of a train transporting a boy to a boarding school

Sean Smith, *J.K. Rowling: A Biography*. London, UK: Michael O'Mara Books Limited, 2001.

for wizards: 'All of a sudden the idea for Harry just appeared in my mind's eye. I can't tell you why or what triggered it. But I saw the idea of Harry and the wizard school very plainly. I suddenly had this basic idea of a boy who didn't know who he was, who didn't know he was a wizard until he got his invitation to wizard school. I have never been so excited by an idea.'

Rowling Develops Her Idea

Unusually, to her frustration, Joanne had neither pen nor paper with her that June evening so she closed her eyes to see everything inside her own head. She thought about the main character Harry, although she had not set upon his name then. She concentrated on the school and the people Harry might meet there. She told Lindsey Fraser [author of *Telling Tales: An Interview with J.K. Rowling*] that by the end of the journey she had thought of Ron Weasley, based on [Rowling's friend] Séan Harris, Hagrid the gamekeeper, the character she has said she would most like to meet in real life, and the school ghosts Nearly Headless Nick and Peeves. At this early stage she did not have names for all her characters. They would come later using, among other sources, gazetteers and *Brewer's Dictionary of Phrase and Fable.*

Most of all Joanne considered the school itself and what it might be like. She imagined a Scottish setting because Scotland had been important to her parents and parts of it were wild and windy. She thought of a castle but not one in particular she had seen. Hogwarts is a combination of many buildings: Tintern Abbey near Chepstow perhaps, Thomas Hall at Exeter University or a peculiar construction erected for a school project in the main hall at Wyedean when she was thirteen. They all went into the melting pot that became Hogwarts. Later, back in her room, she frantically jotted down what she could remember from the train in a small, cheap, flimsy notebook—the very first Harry Potter document.

To suggest that Harry Potter instantly became an all-consuming passion for Joanne is an exaggeration. At this early stage, June 1990, publication was seven years away. It was, however, a welcome diversion from the tedium of a life that seemed to be going nowhere. She found a temporary secretarial job with the Manchester Chamber of Commerce and by the end of the year had relocated from London to Manchester. It is typical of a person who can leave no footprints that the Chamber of Commerce, despite exhaustive research, can find no record of Joanne ever working there. Staff, including Harry Potter fans, who have been working there for twenty years cannot remember ever meeting her. She also worked for a time at Manchester University.

But there was always the boy wizard to help while away the time and soon her notes on the saga filled a shoebox. Most authors say that this is the best fun in writing, running with the creative baton and seeing where it leads. Joanne had already decided there would be seven books, which some commentators thought arrogant of an unpublished author. But it was purely sensible—one book for each of Harry's years at Hogwarts. She had also settled on the name of her hero. 'Harry has always been my favourite boy's name and Potter was the surname of the family who used to live near me when I was seven. I always liked the name so I borrowed it.' Possible names for other characters would be collected enthusiastically and stored in the box: Dumbledore, for instance, is an Old English word for a bumblebee, and features in *The Mayor of Casterbridge* by Thomas Hardy.

The Death of Her Mother Has a Profound Effect on Rowling

Despite the almost Damascene vision of Harry Potter it was not the most significant event of the year. Anne Rowling [Joanne's mother] died on 30 December 1990. She was forty-five. Joanne had been home to Church Cottage just before

Christmas. 'She was extremely thin and looked exhausted. I don't know how I didn't realize how ill she was, except that I had watched her deteriorate for so long that the change, at the time, didn't seem so dramatic.' Joanne said goodbye to her mother, not realizing it was for the last time, on Christmas Eve and left Tutshill to celebrate the holiday with her boyfriend and his family. On New Year's Eve she was woken at 7.30 a.m. to be told her father was on the phone. That was unheard of and she immediately feared the worst. She instinctively knew what had happened: 'I still can't write about her without crying.' . . .

Her mother's death had a profound effect on Joanne Rowling, one that she continues to acknowledge. It affected the direction of her own life and also the direction of Harry Potter. For a while she became rudderless. She returned miserably to Manchester, to a life that was going nowhere and a relationship that was deteriorating. After one particularly bad row she stormed out to a pub and later booked herself into a small hotel room in Didsbury, a suburb of Manchester.

The evening was not wasted. To take her mind off things Joanne decided it would be fun if they played a particular wizard sport at Hogwarts. She thought of Quidditch, an original game played with more than one ball and with a name which this time came from the recesses of Joanne's imagination and not from an atlas.

When Joanne was trying to think of a first name for young Master Dursley she originally thought of Didsbury, but in the end decided the residents of that Manchester suburb where she devised Quidditch did not deserve to be associated with Harry's ghastly relative. Wanting an alliterative name, Joanne settled on Dudley although only she could know what the people of that West Midlands town had done to warrant 'Dudders,' as Aunt Marge calls him.

Joanne paid the best compliment she could to her mother by writing the chapter 'The Mirror of Erised' in the first Harry

Potter book [*Harry Potter and the Philosopher's Stone*]. It is probably the most famous of all Harry Potter chapters and the one of which Joanne says she is proudest. It is undoubtedly the most moving. The Mirror of Erised is a magical mirror in which the reflection you see is the image you most want to see in the whole world. Dumbledore explains to Harry, 'It shows us nothing more or less than the deepest, most desperate desire of our hearts.'

In Harry's case he sees his dead parents waving. His mother is smiling and crying at the same time: 'He had a powerful kind of ache inside him, half joy, half terrible sadness.' Joanne has admitted: 'When I reread the chapter I saw that I had given Harry lots of my own feelings about my own mother's death.'

If Joanne looked into the Mirror of Erised she would see her mother Anne. She revealed in a magazine interview that she would want five minutes to tell her all the news: 'I'd gabble on and at the end of five minutes I'd realize I hadn't asked what it's like to be dead. It's the selfishness of the child, isn't it?'

From the point of view of plot Harry Potter being an orphan is useful. He does not have parents interfering, he has to fend for himself and he can stay at school during the holiday breaks. To a certain extent Joanne felt that she had been orphaned after her mother died. Her feeling lent a more serious, moral side to Harry as a character. Those who knew Anne Rowling have spotted a debt to her in the first book. [Family friend] John Nettleship observes, 'When I read the books I feel I am always being presented with the values of Anne and Pete Rowling whose standards were very high. Both Joanne's parents had a strong sense of justice and a strong sense of accountability. I regarded them as being of the highest quality and what I love about the books is that they reflect the ethos of her family.

'You can see really that the books emanate from her childhood. It's not that they represent a sort of "I must write this in memory of my mother." It's nothing like that. Joanne has said that when she reread the first book she discovered there was a lot of her mother in that. This is what Shirley and I felt as soon as we read it. You're just aware of her mother in the background and the way her mother would think about things.'

One of the most obvious tributes to Joanne's mother is in the means by which the infant Harry is able to thwart the evil Voldemort. In *The Chamber of Secrets* Harry tells him: 'I know why you couldn't kill me. Because my mother died to save me.' . . .

Rowling Goes to Portugal to Teach English

A small advertisement in the *Guardian* newspaper caught Joanne's eye: 'Qualified English teachers required for a school in Porto.' Joanne had little relevant experience for a teaching job other than her year in Paris but Porto sounded just the sort of place where [author] Jessica Mitford would have ended up. So she sent off a CV, a covering letter explaining her enthusiasm for teaching in Portugal and a contact phone number. The advertisement had been placed by Steve Cassidy, principal of the Encounter English Schools in Porto. The turnover of staff teaching English abroad was quite high, so every year he would seek to employ three or four new teachers, sifted from forty or so replies.

On a trip to England to visit his family in Barnsley he would contact half a dozen applicants and arrange to see them. He met Joanne at a hotel close to the railway station in Leeds. 'We had coffee and chatted,' he recalls. 'She was a bit gothic-looking with very dark eye-shadow. She looked like Morticia from the Addams family. She wasn't an outstanding candidate but I thought she would be OK. She was a bit shy and I remember she looked a bit sad at the station. I think her mother had recently died.' . . .

Joanne got the job. She was thrilled to be starting her own new adventure. . . .

The main hours for classes were from 5 p.m. until 10 p.m. with a couple of hours on Saturday mornings, so there was plenty of time for her to shut the door of the computer room and type up her Harry Potter notes on a word processor. . . .

During the day she could indulge her liking for writing in long hand in coffee bars. Porto is well served in this respect and one in particular, the Café Majestic on rua de Santa Catarina, became a favourite haunt. The Majestic is a tranquil Art Deco oasis of style and flair with white marble table tops, ornate wooden chairs, chandeliers and a grand piano, which is occasionally played. Joanne could sit and smoke, sip her strong Portuguese coffee and dream of wizards. . . .

Rowling Meets Her First Husband

The night that changed Joanne's life began in ordinary fashion. She strolled with [her friends] Aine and Jill to the Labareda for an evening drink. It was a typical Saturday night in March and she had been in Porto for five months. The three friends decided to move on to the Ribeiro to a bar and perhaps a club. They chose the Meia Cava, a place where, according to Maria Inês [Aguiar, assistant director of the school in Portugal where Rowling taught], 'you could go crazy, get drunk and look for love.' It is a few yards back from the river in a little courtyard square littered with tables and chairs where friends and sweethearts unwind with coffee and beers. Meia Cava has a plain dark green door with no name on it. Downstairs was a mellow bar area with jazz music and upstairs a disco. Joanne and the 'godmothers' chose downstairs where, by chance, a young Portuguese journalism student was drinking with friends. 'This girl with the most amazing blue eyes walked in,' he remembers.

J.K. Rowling poses in a New York bookstore in October 1998, about a year after the publication of Harry Potter and the Sorcerer's Stone. AP Images.

Jorge Arantes was unable to take his eyes off Joanne who, with her mane of dark red hair and deep eye-shadow, stood out as different from Portuguese girls. . . .

They realized that evening there could be something more between them than a night of flirting in a bar because they shared a love of books. . . .

Soon the young lovers were spending more nights together than apart. . . . Joanne discovered she was pregnant. It was not the best time for the couple. Jorge had to do eight months' National Service in the Portuguese Army. The couple, who had been together only a short time, decided against a termination. . . .

As Porto became unbearably hot in the summer of 1992, Joanne and Jorge planned a trip to England for a month when she could introduce him to her family and friends and give everyone her good news. That plan was ruined when she suffered a miscarriage, but Jorge maintained this sad event brought the couple closer together: 'We decided that when the time was right, we would try for another baby and also get married.' He proposed on 28 August 1992. . . .

At the same time cracks were appearing in the relationship and one dramatic row reveals how flawed it was even before they had a daughter together, and how turbulent it became. The couple were having an afternoon coffee in the Casa Imperio across the road from the language school. There was no warning of the drama that was about to unfold or what sparked it although Maria Inês comments, 'He was very possessive and jealous.'

An argument exploded into life. Maria Inês recalls that Jorge shoved Joanne, nothing more: 'He pushed her and she screamed.' Joanne ran into the street screaming and shouting pursued by a still irate Jorge. Maria Inês remembers, 'She ran into our building and up the stairs into Room Two. A big crowd gathered in the street because they thought he was going to do for her. He had that look.' . . .

Within a few weeks [after her wedding to Jorge in October 1992] Joanne was pregnant again. It was a fretful time because of her previous miscarriage, but the pregnancy proved undramatic. She spent more time than ever working on her Harry Potter notes and her friends at the Encounter English School noticed she was more isolated than before, often sitting in the local cafés by herself. . . .

Joanne's daughter was born on 27 July 1993 in the Maternidade Júlio Dinis nursing home after a seven-hour labour and her parents called her Jessica. Joanne described the birth as 'without doubt the best moment of my life.' A boy would have been called Harry. . . .

By November the marriage had reached breaking point. One evening another row erupted which once again led to a scene of high drama in the street. . . .

Rowling Returns to Scotland and Applies for Welfare

Her [Joanne's] plan was simple. First it was to escape from Porto with her daughter. This had been achieved [in the autumn of 1993]. They would be a lot more secure in her home country than in Portugal, where she was unsure of how the law [regarding divorce and child custody] might work. She needed to find a place to live and, in the New Year, a job, ideally teaching. She had very little money, enough to rent somewhere for a couple of months. Her friends in London had moved on so she resolved to try her luck in Edinburgh where her sister Di had settled happily. . . .

Di has the happy knack of looking on the bright side and she would always encourage her sister, most importantly in the progress of Harry Potter. Joanne later recalled telling her sister about Harry for the first time while at Marchmont Road. She had left Porto with the first three chapters written and notes on the rest of the first book and many more ideas for the remainder of the series, including the conclusion. Di persuaded Joanne to let her see what she had written so far and was instantly hooked. 'It's possible if she had not laughed, I would have set the whole thing to one side,' admits Joanne, 'but Di did laugh.' . . .

To compound her misery Joanne had to face the nightmare of bureaucracy. On 21 December 1993, she found herself relating her unfortunate circumstances to the Department of Social Security in Commercial Street, in the district of Leith. She had to fill in form upon form to claim income support and housing benefit. She described her ordeal with candour: 'You have to be interviewed and explain to a lot of strangers how you came to be penniless and the sole carer of your child. I know that nobody was setting out to make me feel humiliated and worthless, though that is exactly how I felt.' . . .

Joanne found herself slipping deeper into a depression—not a flatness, or a sadness, or a sighing 'I'm feeling a bit down today,' but a deep black hole of despair. The Dementors, which appear for the first time in *The Prisoner of Azkaban*, are the creative result from a period of her life which she said was the most unpleasant thing she had ever experienced: 'It is that absence of being able to envisage that you will ever be able to be cheerful again, the absence of hope, that very deadened feeling which is so very different from feeling sad.'

The Dementors are the prison guards of Azkaban and a metaphor for depression itself. In tandem with The Mirror of Erised they represent the most personal aspect of the Harry Potter books so far and may be part of the proof that it is Joanne Rowling herself who is Harry Potter. She may be Hermione Granger, school swot and know-all, but she is also Harry, a child who misses his mother, who hates being the object of attention and gossip and who crumbles in the presence of a Dementor. With a kiss from the gaping, shapeless hole of a mouth a Dementor will suck the happiness out of people and take their souls. Despite their grimness it is an amusing touch that the antidote to the dreadful feelings brought on by the Dementor is, as every woman knows, chocolate. . . .

Rowling Finishes Harry Potter in a Coffee Shop

Somehow, the first summer after leaving Porto, Joanne started slowly to turn things around. The changes that were happening were not all for the worse. On 10 August 1994 she filed for divorce. Perhaps nine months of counselling helped but for the first time since her flight back from Portugal she started to think of plans and fill her days with something more than Dementors. Her brother-in-law Roger had formed The Sint Partnership with a friend called Dougal McBride and they had bought a not terribly fashionable café called Nicolson's near the junction of South Bridge and the Royal Mile. It was to prove a purchase of some significance for Joanne. She still wanted to write Harry Potter and her desire to tell stories and be a professional writer was as strong as ever. The height of her ambition was to hand her credit card to someone in a shop and for them to tell her that she had written their favourite book, but it was never going to happen in South Lorne Place.

She needed somewhere to go where she would not feel lonely or isolated but would be in the company of people leading their own lives who would leave her alone to pursue her own. Coffee houses had been a source of inspiration since her days working in London and later in Porto, but on her less than meagre budget she could not afford to spend afternoons drinking cup after cup of designer coffee. Nicolson's was a godsend. It was in the family so the staff would be sympathetic to her nursing the same cup of coffee for an hour, sometimes two, at a time. Fate may have been giving her a sign because one street away from Nicolson's is a road called Potterrow.

Joanne would set off with Jessica in her buggy and walk the half-hour along Easter Road to the centre of town. If she was lucky Jessica would be asleep by the time they reached South Bridge. If she was still awake, then Joanne would wheel her up the Royal Mile past the exotically named lanes that looked down on the rooftops of houses below. It is a very atmospheric part of the city and relatively unspoilt despite the bagpipe music that fills the air in this tourist trap part of town. Many places could claim inspiration for Diagon Alley, the shopping street for wizards in the Harry Potter stories. But few have a better case than Old Assembly Close, Anchor Close, Old Stamp Office Close and the many other narrow passages of Edinburgh's old town.

When Jessica was soundly asleep Joanne would walk over to Nicolson's and struggle up the twenty steps to the first floor and try to find a quiet corner table to work on her Harry Potter notes. Nicolson's had a cheap and cheerful studenty feel to it with a blue and yellow colour scheme, a selection of [Henri] Matisse prints on the wall and distinctive Art Deco windows and lighting. Ideally Jessica would stay asleep while Joanne worked. At least in Nicolson's it felt as if she had a life. One afternoon a week a girlfriend would take Jessica for a couple of hours, and Joanne would be able to have a break, read a novel—she liked [Vladimir] Nabokov and Roddy Doyle—or work on the rules of Quidditch. . . .

Rowling Gets an Agent

Bryony Evens opened the mail in the offices of the Christopher Little Literary Agency in Walham Grove, Fulham. It was a freezing February morning with nothing on the horizon to brighten the day. . . .

Fortunately for Joanne Rowling, Bryony loved to read, especially classic children's literature. . . . If Joanne could have handpicked someone to look at Harry Potter, then she could have done no better than Bryony who, at twenty-five, was the same age Joanne had been when she first thought up the schoolboy wizard.

The majority of the submitted scripts would go straight into the reject basket and that was where Harry Potter first went on that February morning. It was not because Bryony did not care for the manuscript. *Harry Potter and the Philosopher's Stone* was obviously a children's book and the agency did not handle them. . . . The good news for Joanne was that Bryony always had a flick through the reject basket later before sorting out things for return. She noticed Harry Potter at lunchtime because of the unusual black plastic wallet Joanne had used.

'I fished it out to take a look. There was a synopsis and three sample chapters, which was what we asked to be sent in as standard. The first thing I noticed was that there were illustrations with it. There was one of Harry standing by the fireplace in the Dursleys' house with his scruffy hair and the lightning scar on his forehead. I started reading the first chapter and it was almost identical to how it was eventually published. The main thing that struck me, because I loved it, was the humour: when Mrs Dursley tells Mr Dursley that Dudley had learnt a new word "Shan't"." Bryony finished the first chapter and was sufficiently impressed to put the manuscript to one side to finish the remaining two later.

At the time the agency employed a young freelance reader, Fleur Howle, to look at unsolicited manuscripts and to work with authors on those they liked, to make sure they were of a high enough standard for submission to publishers. Fleur came into the office that afternoon and Bryony passed over Joanne's manuscript. 'This looks really good,' she said. 'I've read the first chapter and I'm going to read the rest later but do you want to read it now to see what you think?' Fleur read the whole submission and, like Bryony, was impressed. 'To be completely accurate,' recalls Bryony, 'I read the first chapter first and Fleur read chapters two and three first. At the end of the day I read them too and said to Chris [Christopher Little] "Can we send off for it?" and he said, "Yes, whatever." And that was it.' . . .

Bloomsbury Agrees to Publish Harry Potter

It was time for *Harry Potter and the Philosopher's Stone* to be sent to a publisher. . . .

In all some twelve publishers turned down the chance to publish J.K. Rowling until a manuscript was sent to the offices of Bloomsbury in Soho Square. . . . Bloomsbury had recently started up a children's book division under Barry Cunningham, who had moved into editing from marketing and, like Christopher Little, had a flair for the business potential of a project.

Barry's ambition was to publish books which 'children would respond to' and he instantly found that quality in *The Philosopher's Stone*. 'It was just terribly exciting. What struck me first was that the book came with a fully imagined world.

There was a complete sense of Jo knowing the characters and what would happen to them. It was, however, very long for a children's book at that time.' . . .

Eventually, after about a month, Barry was able to make an offer of £1,500 ($2,250). . . . Christopher sorted out the finer points of the contract personally and advised Joanne to accept the offer. . . .

Bloomsbury made arrangements for Joanne to come to London and meet everyone for lunch. . . .

Lunch was at a little Soho brasserie, which gave Joanne the opportunity to pop into the famous Hamley's toy store in Regent Street to buy a present for Jessica. Barry Cunningham thought it a great lunch. 'I thought she was shy about herself but very confident and intense about the book and, most importantly, confident that children would like Harry. I knew she had had a tough time since coming back from Portugal so I was very impressed with her dedication to the story. She just so understood about growing up.' At the end of lunch Barry shook the hand of his latest author and told her, 'You'll never make any money out of children's books, Jo.' The remark has become one of Joanne's favourite stories.

Social Issues in Literature

Chapter 2

Harry Potter and Political Issues

The Harry Potter Books Critique Bureaucracy

Benjamin H. Barton

Benjamin H. Barton, an associate professor of law at the University of Tennessee College of Law, believes that the popularity of the Harry Potter books makes an examination of Rowling's views on government worthwhile. Barton theorizes that Rowling is using the Ministry of Magic to represent her own view on governmental institutions. The Ministry of Magic is portrayed as corrupt and bureaucratic, argues Barton, and it bears a strong resemblance to the British and U.S. governments. He concludes by surmising that Rowling's views on bureaucracy were shaped by her experience on public assistance, and he speculates that she may be supportive of the libertarian movement.

What would you think of a government that engaged in this list of tyrannical activities: tortured children for lying; designed its prison specifically to suck all life and hope out of the inmates; placed citizens in that prison without a hearing; ordered the death penalty without a trial; allowed the powerful, rich, or famous to control policy; selectively prosecuted crimes (the powerful go unpunished and the unpopular face trumped-up charges); conducted criminal trials without defense counsel; used truth serum to force confessions; maintained constant surveillance over all citizens; offered no elections and no democratic lawmaking process; and controlled the press?

You might assume that the above list is the work of some despotic central African nation, but it is actually the product of the Ministry of Magic, the magicians' government in J.K. Rowling's Harry Potter series. . . .

Given the overwhelming popularity and influence of the Harry Potter books, it is worth examining what Rowling has to say about government and its role in society. [The first part of this essay] gives a short synopsis of the plot and themes of *The Half-Blood Prince* and its predecessors, and describes how *The Half-Blood Prince* cements Rowling's negative portrayal of government. [The second part of this essay] argues that *The Half-Blood Prince* presents a government that fits perfectly into the public-choice model of self-interested bureaucrats running roughshod over the broader public interest. [The third part of this essay] asserts that *The Half-Blood Prince*'s unflattering depiction of government is particularly damning because it so closely resembles the British and U.S. governments, but without many of the features that potentially undermine the public-choice critique. Rowling's vision of government consists almost solely of bureaucracy, without elections to offer the sheen of democracy, without a free press or independent judiciary to act as a check on bureaucratic excess, and with few true public servants to counteract craven bureaucrats. [The fourth part of this essay] talks a little bit about how Rowling's personal story may explain her disdain for government and bureaucracy. [The fifth part] concludes that Rowling may do more for libertarianism than anyone since [the ninteenth-century philosopher and economist] John Stuart Mill.

Harry Potter and the Repulsive Ministry of Magic

Rowling's Harry Potter books, up to and including *The Half-Blood Prince*, slowly but surely build an impregnable invective against government, while still telling charming fantasy stories about witches and wizards at a school for magic. Each of the first six Harry Potter books follows a similar template. They begin with Harry Potter living with his extremely unlikable "muggle" relations. They then proceed through the course of a school year at the Hogwarts School of Witchcraft and Wizardry. Each year presents a new mystery to be resolved or a Lord Voldemort-inspired challenge to overcome, as well as the details of Harry's social life and school work.

The last three books all have the same meta-narrative: Lord Voldemort has returned from the dead, and is seeking to kill Harry and take over the world. Book four, *The Goblet of Fire*, ends with Voldemort's return to full power (and the murder of fellow student Cedric Diggory). In book five, *The Order of the Phoenix*, Voldemort tries to discover the exact contents of the prophesy that proclaims that either Harry or Voldemort are destined to kill the other. In *The Half-Blood Prince*, Harry and the Hogwarts headmaster—and Harry's hero—Professor Dumbledore explore the history and nature of Voldemort, presumably in preparation for Harry's final battle against Voldemort in the next, and final, book in the series.

The first five books lay the groundwork for Rowling's depiction of the Ministry of Magic in *The Half-Blood Prince*. The first three books take a relatively lighthearted view of the wizard government. Rowling gives us goofy and highly bureaucratic-sounding government offices like "[t]he Misuse of Muggle Artifacts Office" or "the Department of Magical Catastrophes" and a portrait of the Minister of Magic, Cornelius Fudge, as a bumbling, but well-meaning, political hack.

In *The Goblet of Fire*, we have the first real hints of Rowling's darker vision for the Ministry of Magic. The depiction of how the Ministry handles Voldemort's first rise to power features overzealous prosecutions and the suspension of civil rights. Most notably, at the end of the book, the Ministry refuses to believe that Voldemort has returned to power, and actually works to discredit and suppress Harry's story.

The end of *The Goblet of Fire* presages the open hostility between the Ministry of Magic and Harry and Dumbledore in *The Order of the Phoenix*. The Ministry attempts to kick Harry out of school, strips Dumbledore of his various government positions (including headmaster of Hogwarts), sicks the evil-bureaucrat par excellence Dolores Umbridge on Hogwarts, and generally brings the full weight of the Ministry's powers to bear upon Harry and Dumbledore.

Nevertheless, *The Order of the Phoenix* ends on a hopeful note: Fudge finally recognizes that Voldemort has returned to power. We are left with the impression that Fudge will now use the full powers of the Ministry to battle Voldemort and his followers, the Death Eaters. After all, even the most hardened libertarian generally recognizes that government is best suited to fight wars against aggressors and pursue police actions against those who threaten the well-being of others.

The Half-Blood Prince, however, offers no such succor to government. The Ministry remains remarkably ineffective in its battle against Voldemort. Cornelius Fudge is replaced as Minister of Magic by Rufus Scrimgeour, a savvy veteran of the battles against Lord Voldemort, and yet the tone and actions of the Ministry remain unchanged. In fact, Scrimgeour decides to try to calm the public by detaining individuals who are likely innocent. And his attempts to use Harry as a "mascot" or "poster boy" for the ministry are also arguably worse than Fudge's actions.

Perhaps *The Half-Blood Prince*'s most devastating criticism of the Ministry has little to do with Voldemort, however. It is what service in the Ministry of Magic has done to Percy Weasley. Harry's best friend at Hogwarts is Ron Weasley, a member of a large and likable magical family that informally adopts Harry as their own. Percy Weasley is Ron's older brother, and throughout the first three books he is depicted as a bit of a rule-loving stuffed shirt. But the portrait is sympathetic, and it is clear that he is still a lovable member of the Weasley family.

In *The Goblet of Fire*, Percy goes to work for the Ministry of Magic in a junior capacity, and at once finds a home for his love of rules and talent for minutiae. In *The Order of the Phoenix*, however, Percy takes the side of the Ministry against Harry and Dumbledore and ends up alienating his entire family as a result. This offers the first object lesson in government service: Percy essentially loses his soul and all that should matter to him by following his blind ambition.

The Half-Blood Prince, however, offers Percy a chance at redemption. Now that the Ministry recognizes that Voldemort has returned and that Harry is its best chance of defeating him, Percy could admit he was wrong about Dumbledore and Harry and rejoin the family. Yet, Percy refuses to bend and remains estranged. Of course that does not free Percy from the clutches of the government. The first encounter between Harry and Scrimgeour occurs at the Weasley family Christmas dinner, which Scrimgeour crashes with Percy as his excuse. The violation of the Weasley family, and Scrimgeour's callous use of Percy to gain access to Harry, are hardly lost on the readers. The depths that Scrimgeour and Percy will plumb to co-opt Harry are more offensive and distasteful than even the list of government wrongdoing that began this Review, because we experience them directly through the eyes of Harry and the Weasley family.

This is likewise true when Scrimgeour reiterates his request to Harry at the Hogwarts funeral that ends the book. We fully sympathize with Harry's refusal to help the Ministry; how could he do otherwise? Thus, the replacement of Fudge with Scrimgeour and the hardening of Harry's negative feelings toward the Ministry finalize Rowling's portrait of the Ministry of Magic and its bureaucrats. Before *The Half-Blood Prince*, it was possible to imagine that the Ministry of Magic was trying hard, but was misguided or ineffectual. After *The Half-Blood Prince*, the reader reaches the inexorable conclusion that Harry (and Rowling for that matter) has little use for government.

Harry Potter and the Public-Choice Government

The odd thing about Rowling's Ministry of Magic is how closely it accords with the public-choice critique of government. The central tenet of public-choice theory is that the best way to understand the actions of governmental actors is to assume they are primarily—or solely—motivated by self-interest. The theory has been applied to the actions and incentives of virtually every government actor and sector, but it seems to have been most popular as an explanation of bureaucratic behavior. One of the earliest public-choice scholars, William Niskanen, theorized that self-interested bureaucrats would seek to expand their budgets and influence at the expense of the public. This theory has since spawned a cottage industry of public-choice analyses of bureaucracy.

The greatest strength of the public-choice theory is, of course, its simplicity, and how much it comports with our own experience of government. The word "bureaucrat" itself has come to have a negative connotation, and many would instinctively agree that bureaucrats look out for their own interests ahead of the interests of the public.

The power of Rowling's portrait of bureaucratic activity is similarly its believability. Given the list of Ministry of Magic activities at the start of this Review, this is no mean feat. Rowling makes the Ministry's actions reasonable with well-drawn characters and difficult situations. Fudge, the original Minister of Magic, is portrayed as a classic bumbling politician: not quite up to the job, but generally genial and harmless. Fudge's replacement, Scrimgeour, is described as the battle-hardened leader offering "an immediate impression of shrewdness and toughness". Dolores Umbridge is the über-bureaucrat, an unctuous climber who begins every discussion with a phony "Hem Hem" and ends each with multiple references to Ministry protocols. Percy Weasley is the familiar young striver, willing to adopt any position of the Ministry in order to get ahead.

Combining these characters, different in every way except for their overweening self-interest, with the extreme circumstances of the return of Voldemort, the reader believes that the Ministry is capable of almost anything. Furthermore, anyone who has lived in England or the United States post-9/11 will recognize the themes raised by *The Half-Blood Prince*: government by and for the public relations effect, the indefinite detention of suspects for show, obtrusive governmental searches, and government pamphlets offering silly advice of little help. Meanwhile, there is little in the way of actual help.

The most powerful aspect of Rowling's portrait of the Ministry of Magic as a corrupt, self-perpetuating bureaucracy is how natural it all seems. Rowling creates a government that fits—and actually exceeds—each of the public-choice assumptions about government, and closely resembles our own government in personnel and activities.

Harry Potter and the Bureaucracy That Ate Government Whole

Despite the intuitive power of public-choice theory, defenders of government and bureaucracy remain unconvinced, and offer a spirited critique of public-choice theory. Interestingly, Rowling foresees many of these defenses of government, and her portrayal of the Ministry of Magic parries them with ease.

The Democratic Defense. The first line of attack against public-choice theory is always that bureaucrats must answer to elected officials, who must in turn answer to the voters. This defense has both descriptive and normative aspects. As a descriptive/empirical matter, defenders of bureaucracy question whether bureaucrats really have the ability or capacity to hoodwink elected executives or legislators who have to answer to their constituents. As a normative matter, defenders of bureaucracy argue that democracy justifies bureaucracy as a result of deliberation and public buy-in.

Rowling strips the Ministry of Magic of even this most basic justification, as Fudge is replaced by Scrimgeour as the Minister of Magic with no mention of an election. To the contrary, Rowling uses the passive voice of the verb "to sack" repeatedly to describe Fudge's fate. The lack of an election is highlighted by a meeting between the muggle Prime Minister (presumably Tony Blair) and Fudge (the former Minister of Magic) and Scrimgeour (the new Minister). The description of the muggle Prime Minister features a discussion of elections and political opponents, two elements of governmental life that are notably absent from the Ministry of Magic.

One mystery that remains after *The Half-Blood Prince* is the legislative or rule-making power of the Ministry of Magic. It is clear that the Ministry enforces the laws, and there are discussions in the books about adopting new laws, but there is never any mention of a legislature or legislative process. The hints that Rowling drops, however, are not encouraging.

These omissions are purposeful, authorial decisions by Rowling. A government that has no elections and no democratic process for lawmaking obviously lacks the legitimacy of a democratic regime. Nevertheless, the overall similarity of the Ministry of Magic to our own government in actions, motivation, and personnel suggests that elections and democratic lawmaking actually have little, if any, effect on government as experienced by it subjects.

The Structural Defense. Defenders of bureaucracy frequently note that bureaucrats are overseen by other governmental and nongovernmental entities. In the U.S. system, for example, bureaucrats are subject to varying levels of oversight by the president, Congress, a politically appointed head of the agency, and a free press to root out any wrongdoing.

The first thing to note about Rowling's Ministry of Magic is that she has created a government structure that appears to be one hundred percent bureaucracy. There is a Minister of Magic, but he is appointed, not elected. It is unclear who appoints the Minister of Magic, but perhaps it is the elites. There are multiple offices and committees below the Minister, but each of these appears to be a classic bureaucracy within a bureaucracy, each staffed by a junior minister with their own area of responsibility.

There is a judicial body, the Wizengamot, which Rowling describes as the "the Wizard High Court." We have good reason to believe it is substantially controlled by the Minister of Magic, and it certainly does not seem to be an independent check on Ministry authority.

There are thus no governmental bodies outside the Ministry of Magic to act as a check upon government abuses. Again, this suggests that neither governmental structure nor checks and balances matter much: bureaucracy will run roughshod regardless.

The Free Press. Free speech and freedom of the press are generally taken as constitutional guarantees in the United States, and are perceived to be fundamental to a just and responsive government. In the narrower sense, a free press is considered another check on bureaucratic or governmental misconduct.

Humorously, Rowling denies the magical world a free press (or even a functional press). Both *The Half-Blood Prince* and *The Order of the Phoenix* are replete with instances of the Ministry leaning on the press to print what is essentially government propaganda. Again, this strips the government of even the possibility of press oversight, or realistically public oversight, because wizards (not unlike we poor muggles) typically rely upon the press for information outside of their daily experience.

Bureaucrats Are People Too. Another line of defense is the public-minded bureaucrat. Some theorists argue that the public-choice critique ignores what government officials are really like. They are not greedy, self-interested, budget-maximizers. Instead, they are decent and publicly oriented.

Rowling rolls over this possibility in three ways. There are five main characters that are Ministry employees: Fudge, Scrimgeour, Umbridge, Percy Weasley, and Arthur Weasley (Ron and Percy's father). The first four of these five characters are basically villains, and are unquestionably motivated by self-interest and a naked lust for power rather than the public interest. The fifth of those characters, Arthur Weasley, is actually the exception that proves the rule. He is a decent, hard-working bureaucrat who loves his work at the Ministry. Of course, in Rowling's Ministry, no good deed goes unpunished. Arthur Weasley is described as a relative failure. At one point in *The Order of the Phoenix*, Harry is taken to his office, which is in the basement, down several long hallways, and is "slightly smaller than [a] broom cupboard." Lastly, in *The Half-Blood Prince*, two of the most revered characters, Dumbledore and Harry, clearly have little use for the Ministry or its bureaucrats.

Love It or Leave It. There is not a strong scholarly tradition of what I am calling the "love it or leave it" defense, but it does exist, and has actually come to the fore in recent years. This defense of government basically requires citizens to accept the legitimacy of the government and its actions as a duty of citizenship, and then rebukes any criticisms as unpatriotic. The interesting thing about this defense is that it explicitly raises the question of governmental legitimacy: if one assumes governmental legitimacy, it may be appropriate to ask a citizen to "love it or leave it." If one leaves open the possibility that governments and laws may lack legitimacy, it becomes much harder simply to order blind allegiance.

Rowling makes quick work of this potential defense. In *The Half-Blood Prince*, Harry makes it clear that he feels no independent duty to be used by the Ministry for the benefit of the public. Harry's decision should come as no surprise:

throughout the novels Harry seems to pick and choose certain school rules—and even Ministry laws—to follow or disregard depending on the situation and his own sense of morality or duty. Rowling treats these decisions by Harry as if they are natural and easy, but taken together with Harry's rejection of the Ministry's overtures in *The Half-Blood Prince*, Rowling presents a remarkably contingent and situational approach to both government and law.

In sum, Rowling has created a world where all of our negative governmental stereotypes have come true. She combines familiar character types and government structures with a vision of government by the bureaucrats, and for the bureaucrats, to create a devastating critique of Anglo-American government.

J.K. Rowling and the Libertarian Mind-set

Anyone familiar with Rowling's personal story will know that when she started the Harry Potter series, she spent a period of time unemployed and on public assistance in Edinburgh, divorced with a young child. These biographic details are frequently juxtaposed with Rowling's current financial status.

Rowling's personal story provides two insights into her feelings toward government. First, in both England and the United States there is no quicker route to hating the government than dealing with the various bureaucracies that handle public assistance. As a general rule, you can predict how user-friendly a bureaucracy will be by determining whether the served constituency regularly votes and/or gives campaign contributions. Those persons unfortunate enough to have to rely upon the government for assistance obviously are unlikely to have sufficient funds to donate to political causes. Similarly, poor people are less likely to vote than other socioeconomic groups. As such, you can expect that the bureaucracies set up to deal with the poor will be relatively badly run and user-unfriendly. . . .

Thus, I think that Rowling's experience on public assistance likely soured her on bureaucracy for a lifetime.

Second, Rowling's story smacks of success through self-reliance and sheer force of will. The Harry Potter novels likewise show a strong strain of self-reliance and stubborn independence, and Rowling came upon these themes the hard way. Anyone who has pulled herself out of poverty as Rowling has is likely to believe that self-reliance and hard work are the keys to success, and to be conversely wary of government intervention.

Harry Potter and the Future Libertarian Majority

The Libertarian Party claims to be the fastest-growing political party in the United States. After reading *The Half-Blood Prince,* I am much more convinced. The libertarian movement relies upon two interrelated concepts to recruit: (a) "that government is best which governs least;" and (b) self-reliance and respect of individual rights should be paramount. *The Half-Blood Prince* makes both of these points exceptionally well. Rowling taps into the current general distrust of government in the United States and the United Kingdom and creates a Ministry of Magic that simultaneously echoes and critiques our own governments. On the one hand, she creates a government that is repulsive in its structure, personnel, and actions. On the other, she crafts this government to appear closely related to our own government. This juxtaposition creates a powerful and subtle critique of government.

The truly surprising aspect of *The Half-Blood Prince* is how effortlessly Rowling covers the questions of the nature, role, and legitimacy of government in what is ostensibly a work of children's literature. I must admit that when I sat down to reread the Harry Potter books in light of *The Half-Blood Prince* I did not expect to find the overwhelming skepticism of government that seeps through Rowling's work. Of course, the ability to entertain first and foremost, although providing other levels of discourse, is the hallmark of great and thoughtful literature, and *The Half-Blood Prince* is both.

The Harry Potter Books Exemplify Tony Blair's New Labour Politics

Jeremy Gilbert

Jeremy Gilbert, lecturer in cultural studies at the University of East London, argues that the Harry Potter books are both a commentary on and representative of the politics of former U.K. prime minister Tony Blair. The values of the novels, Gilbert asserts, are those of the politically centrist Blair administration: multicultural tolerance, liberal individualism, capitalism, and social justice. Gilbert is the author of Cultural Capitalism: Politics After New Labour.

However far is the journey from Hogwarts to No. 10 Downing Street [the office and residence of the prime minister of the United Kingdom], *Harry Potter* is a representative figure of the Blairite age that began with the election of New Labour to power in 1997. That is not to decry the straightforward enjoyability that derives from the books' clever employment of every narrative cliché imaginable, nor to deny that their huge success is itself an important cultural phenomenon. Rather, it is to propose that the books can be read as both commentary and exemplification of the distinct political moment of Tony Blair's core aspiration: the creation of a "Third Way" in which a new combination of social concern and commercial entrepreneurship underpins the social order (or keeps the show on the road, as the more sceptical would see it).

The world of the Third Way (or whatever other name we want to give to the political strategy of parties formerly known as socialist), is governed by a clearly technocratic agenda.

Jeremy Gilbert, "Harry Potter and the Third Way," openDemocracy.net, November 28, 2001. Reproduced by permission.

Think tanks and policy units develop technical solutions to social problems, in consultation with focus groups and press secretaries: the processes of political democracy are bypassed entirely by the rule of the "techno-managerial elite". All this bears a striking resemblance to the world of adult wizards and witches in which the *Harry Potter* stories are set. The parallel society inhabited by wizards in Rowling's world is a perfect Blairite technocracy, governed by a "ministry of magic" (i.e. a ministry of pure science, of *techne* as such) in which almost every adult who is not engaged in either teaching or commerce is employed, and which seems to administer without any formal process of consultation.

The Multicultural Embrace

There are two other elements of *Harry Potter* that chime in well with the British experience of Blairism. The first and perhaps the most pressing contemporary concern in the books is that of cultural difference. In J.K. Rowling's universe, witches and wizards occupy an alternative society, inhabiting the same chronology and geographical space as non-magical people ("muggles") but sharing a very different history. Muggle technology, and even more muggle politics and economics, is as mysterious and irrelevant to wizards as magic is to muggles. However, the boundaries between the two communities are not entirely clear. Magical ability appears to be genetic, such that the children of witches and wizards will almost always possess it, where the children of muggles very rarely will (when they do, they are invited to enrol at a magical academy and thereby to enter into magical society). This encourages most magicals to marry only within the community, and gives rise to a degree of prejudice amongst its less enlightened members towards those born partly or entirely of muggle parentage. "Mudblood" is the name given to the latter, but it is only the evil characters in the book who will use such racist language.

By the same token, Harry Potter's muggle family—his uncle, aunt and cousin—hate, fear and despise his magical life and friends. These characters are drawn as identikit Roald Dahl villains: over-fed, over-privileged conformists whose hatred of difference is inseparable from their sadism towards the long-suffering Harry. In either case, intolerance and ethnic purism are presented as inherent evils in a clear allegory of contemporary multiculturalism.

The Neoliberal Gloss

Roald Dahl villains his tormentors may be, but Harry Potter is no Charlie Bucket [the title character of Dahl's novel *Charlie and the Chocolate Factory*]. This good-hearted orphan boy turns out to be a messianic figure in the wizard world, and a very rich one to boot. However, he never uses the ample supply of gold stashed in the wizard bank, Gringotts, to do anything so radical as to help his best friend and surrogate family. While the poverty of Ron Weasley and his kin is a constant theme of the books, the possibility of Harry sharing his inherited fortune with them is raised only to be dismissed on the grounds that they would never accept it. Yet Ron's elder brothers do accept a business start-up grant from Harry (a gift of 1000 coins to start a joke shop).

Now, if Harry were a character from an earlier generation of children's fiction he would probably have spent, say, half of the second book devising a way of giving away his money without the recipients knowing. Such gratuitous generosity has no place in Harry's new world. This is a "community" in which even wizards still need currency—and where the character who works for the bank is the only adult described as "cool". In his pony tail and dragon-hide boots, Bill Weasley assures his fretful mother that "no-one at the bank gives a damn how I dress as long as I bring home plenty of treasure". Thus, multicultural tolerance and individualist liberalism co-exist happily with finance capital and gross inequalities of wealth, which should only be overcome to the extent that all are enabled to take part in the adventure of business. Welcome to Blair's world.

Education, Education, Specialisation

Hogwarts, *Harry Potter*'s imaginary school for young wizards, is not simply an old-fashioned boarding school—open to anyone from the right class—with magic on the curriculum. Nor, obviously, is it a comprehensive [a school in the United Kingdom that corresponds to a high school in the United States]. More appropriately, the books' eponymous hero attends a school which is selective and specialised: choosing students for their talent and training them intensively in their assigned vocation. Here again, Harry is presented to us as a boy for our times, even a mythical embodiment of all the priorities and prejudices which constitute the New Labour 'structure of feeling': a truly Blairite hero.

Where there is direct 'political' intervention in the books, it follows the script perfectly. When Hermione, the muggle-born feminist swot [British slang for a person who studies too much] of the school tries to organise the long-suffering house-elves to resist their condition of perpetual enslavement, her campaign is met with mockery and indifference; even the house-elves themselves don't want to be free. What actually happens is that *one* elf, the quasi-heroic Dobby (having learned to live with freedom and to demand wages for his work) comes to stay at Hogwarts. Hermione gives up on her campaign to organise the elves or her class mates, but resigns herself to the possibility that Dobby's example may slowly raise their consciousness. It is a perfect allegory of incremental, Blairite centrism.

But what is perhaps most significant about *Harry Potter* is the particular elements of older types of tale which it chooses to retain for contemporary consumption. What is emphasised again and again in the books is not simply the ordinariness of

Harry's aspirations, but his historical uniqueness. It is true that Harry's is a world in which the echoes of older value systems—ones favouring community, justice, sharing, democracy, as well as conformism, elitism, aristocracy and racism—can still be strongly heard. Nonetheless, it is also a world in which the way to succeed is to exploit one's talents, engage in specialised training, and bring home plenty of treasure. Other paths to fulfilment are almost certainly blocked; but in Harry's world as in Tony's, as long as you don't go making trouble with the house elves, at least no-one will care what you wear.

Be Yourself—and Trust Your Teachers

It would be unfair to pretend that this was the whole story. Hermione, the activist, is a sympathetic character who very rarely turns out to be wrong, in a world where errors of judgement pave the way to damnation. What's more, the books are clearly written from a boy's perspective, and the boys' gradual realisation that Hermione is not just a swotty [nerdy] mate to be called on when library research is needed (one of the series' more interesting literary aspects) may yet come to encompass a more sympathetic attitude to her political radicalism in later volumes.

The only character who turns out more often to be right is the saintly Dumbledore, headmaster of Hogwarts. It is Dumbledore who runs his school as he sees fit, ignoring the disapproval of the ministry when he hires non-conformists to teach in their own ways. It is Dumbledore who volunteers to employ Dobby the house-elf on a living wage, with full holiday rights. It is Dumbledore who regards any official complicity with aristocratic or racist prejudice as insupportable. If any moral message comes home strongly from the *Harry Potter* books, it is not just "be yourself" (the classic exhortation of liberal individualism), but "trust your teachers (more than the government, more than your family, more even than your mates)".

The World of Harry Potter Mirrors Traditional British Liberalism

Barry Rubin

In the following selection, Barry Rubin praises J.K. Rowling for rejecting political correctness in the Harry Potter books. He contends that Rowling depicts a traditional British culture in these books, but a culture that is open to those of other backgrounds and races. Rubin considers the world of Harry Potter most analogous to democratic pluralism, a form of liberalism prevalent in Britain beginning in the 1950s. He believes that, throughout history, the most successful societies have been those governed on the principles of democratic pluralism. Rubin is director of the Global Research in International Affairs (GLORIA) Center at the Interdisciplinary Center in Herzliya, Israel.

Since the Harry Potter series is so wildly and universally popular it is surprising that there has not been more examination of its sociology and cultural politics. It is rather out of step with the unfortunate times through which we are now passing. All the better for Harry Potter and his friends; all the worse for us.

None of the following in any way is intended to suggest that Joanne Kathleen Rowling consciously set out to make the points mentioned below or even agrees with them. But this article draws on the text of the book based on a simple traditional analysis to understand what the text actually says rather than an imaginative imposed "deconstruction" to distort it.

Barry Rubin, "The Politics and Philosophy of Harry Potter," *Global Politician*, August 25, 2007. Reproduced by permission.

Democratic Pluralism in the World of Harry Potter

In this spirit, Harry Potter is in fact a typical example of traditional liberal—at least as it has been historically defined—democratic pluralism, which I happen to think is the best system and which is preferred today by both real liberals and conservatives.

It is precisely the standard liberalism of the 1950s to 1990s before the current high water mark of leftist encroachment on liberalism. Equally, it is the approach gradually endorsed by conservatives today who perhaps at the beginning were reluctant to accept that view but have ultimately long since done so, despite the effort of contemporary leftists to brand them as some type of fascist, racist, imperialist group.

What the book does, then, and which is a large element of its success, is to present a clear, historic standard culture—the traditional British one—as its norm while simultaneously showing a society in which those of other backgrounds, including races, are welcome and treated equally. It presents equality of genders as the proper order of things without turning this into an ideological obsession. It recognizes the need for protection of citizens and societies but also has a great scepticism of government. This society values freedom of speech and inquiry alongside respect for tradition but also includes openness toward innovation. The restriction of rights by governments in the name of an imposed proper political line (political correctness) is angrily rejected. Societies based on these principles have been the most successful in world history by just about every measurement.

The fact that there is a single "national" culture and standard—a dominant monoculture—goes hand in hand with a total freedom for subcultures. What the citizens of the British "wizard community," as it is called in the book, do on their own time is their own business. This society includes South

Asian, Afro-Caribbean, and Chinese people who play by the same social rules as everyone else.

Of course, the books cover themselves on this point by two aspects in their plot. First, the villains are those obsessed with "pure blood," that is an ancestry unmixed with non-magical (Muggle) people. Several of the most extreme of these magico-fascists are of mixed descent (Voldemort, Snape), a clear reflection of reasonably grounded suspicions that [Hitler's belief that] he had or might have had a Jewish ancestor was a basis for his psychotic antisemitism.

Second, the bad guys seem to hate non-human sentient creatures—centaurs, werewolves, and giants—for example. Actually this is somewhat misleading since they do ally with a majority of those in the latter two categories. The racism of the villains is highlighted though it is not completely accurate. They are not averse to crossing such lines in order to win.

The Potter series' orientation, then, is structured on the great liberal struggle of the age (though of course there were plenty of conservatives in foxholes, too) against fascism in World War Two. In this respect it is like J.R.R. Tolkien's *The Lord of the Rings*, parts of which were actually written during the war when the author's son was serving in the Royal Air Force.

Of equal importance is that the Potter series is a battle for conservation rather than revolution. The characters are fighting to protect their society against revolutionary change rather than to promote it. They are surrounded by those who rationalize surrender but are nonetheless willing to die for the civilization they love. They are courageous in identifying evil in the face of obfuscation and rationalization, despite being vilified in the media and by government.

Because Potter seeks to warn of a threat from a violent evil movement he is branded a murderer, lunatic, and arrogant attention-seeker. Those who do nothing and proclaim threats are imaginary are smugly self-congratulating. They control the mainstream media, law enforcement, and eventually the educational system, excluding alternative opinions. If any of this sounds familiar, well that is for your interpretation.

Parallels Between Harry Potter's World and the Democratic Movement

As a literary work, of course, the Potter series can easily be interpreted in many ways, with readers free to insert who they wish as the villain. Still, there are certain elements that lend themselves most easily as parallels to the contemporary democratic movement in the West in its simultaneous struggle against the obfuscation of existing authoritarian threats and those threats themselves. This is especially true of the refusal of the government and media to face the danger, pretending it does not exist and advocating appeasement. Perhaps the best instance for pointing that out is the Ministry of Magic's refusal (in book 5) to let students learn how to defend themselves from evil magic. The textbook it endorses insists that they only employ defensive measures when attacked by the bad guys, an irresistible satire on political correctness gone mental (as Ron Weasley would probably put it).

One factor that simplifies Rowling's problems in managing the current debates is the lack of religion in the wizard community. This is a delicate matter for her. After all, witches were historically seen in modern-day religions as hostile elements (in medieval Christianity as being in league with the devil). In glorifying witchcraft she has to worry whether contemporary Christians would see the series as antagonistic and campaign against it. Still, this issue seems to have been avoided by her.

Of course, given the high level of secularism in Western society today many readers will not even notice this aspect, simply taking for granted the absence of religion. Equally, by not having religion practiced by the wizards she also avoids all

A scene from the 2001 Warner Brothers film Harry Potter and the Sorcerer's Stone *with Maggie Smith and Daniel Radcliffe, in which the sorting hat is placed upon Harry Potter (Daniel Radcliffe) to determine which part of the school he will belong to.* © Pictorial Press Ltd/Alamy.

sorts of problems. Does Hogwarts School of Wizardry and Witchcraft permit Muslim students to leave class in order to pray? Are there chapels and other places of worship on campus? These kinds of knotty issues do not enter into the series.

Yet there is one way in which she brings in religion and it is a very revealing example. Christmas is officially celebrated at Hogwarts as a major holiday. There are no religious manifestations to this celebration (as is often true in contemporary Britain and other Western societies) but the event is nonetheless still there. This could be viewed as a bow to Christian sensibilities. Still, it is more likely the expression of an intertwining between Christmas (and by extension other elements of Christian thinking and worldview) and British society. Rowling probably simply sees this as so integrated into national culture as to be more a matter of "Britishness" than of religion. Such a concept may not survive the multicultural axe. . . .

The Potter books are actually more restrictive than liberal pluralism, much less radical multiculturalism. All the students wear standard clothing (though the Patil sisters wear saris for the equivalent of the prom), eat standard British food (no pastas or curries in the Hogwarts dining room), and so on. By the multicultural standard applied to everything else, the Potter series could be attacked and called all sorts of names, presumably if it were not so popular and the would-be censors—as they always do—lacked imagination.

Remarkably, there are no foreign languages or cultures studied at Hogwarts. The number of non-British or non-white students is few. Inasmuch as it is imaginary, it is also a nostalgic Britain as it was in the past rather than as it is today. Nevertheless, the Potter series also accepts the democratic liberal pluralist sense of the larger world. While there are cute references to foreign magical communities they are each an expression of traditional national cultures and histories taken from their own distinct folklore and mythology. Thus, for example, the Irish mascot is the leprechaun. It is thus a world built on clear national cultures, each treated with respect (with a bit of gentle British making fun of the French included), but every one an entity in itself. These "nations" do not act in an aggressive manner toward each other (relations are handled by a bureau of magical cooperation) but their citizens unapologetically show pride and confidence in their own national traditions, too.

Within the British magical community there is also an "other" (once again to use the post-modern terminology) but this is a diversity of different species which is legitimized since one cannot expect goblins, centaurs, or mainstream giants to adhere to the same culture as humans. Humans are in control but also restrain themselves, from laws they have made, from exploiting other intelligent life forms. While discrimination is decried, political correctness is equally satirized by Hermione's efforts to help house elves accept her definition of freedom even though they do not want to do so.

Liberal pluralism is also championed by supporting individual rights among non-standard human "minorities" to self-expression: a half-giant's (Hagrid's) right to join human society, a centaur (Firenze, who is cast out by his own tribe because he dares "collaborate" with humans) or a werewolf's (Lupin's) right to teach. In contrast, one could expect multiculturalists to justify the authority's (Ministry of Magic) opposing this wish to acculturate into mainstream society. An authentic werewolf, one can almost hear them saying, should be out running around in the forest biting people rather than denying his true identity to join a human political organization (the Order of the Phoenix), take a potion to stop his transformation (no doubt an Uncle Tom centaur), and teach Defense Against the Dark Arts. These plot points reject the anti-individual rights' multicultural demand that each group of immigrants reject the authority of the dominant culture to remain exactly as they have always been.

Subcultures Exist Within the Framework of a Strong Standard Culture

What we see in the Potter series—and which makes so many people love the novels—is the glory of a strong culture with time-tested clear standards and ideas that it educates citizens to treasure. Individuals have a right to choose; sub-cultures have a right to their own ways within the broader context. Each country has its own mainstream culture and style. Diversity is welcome but is not the ultimate value.

One of many ironies of the opposing view is that the radical vision of multiculturalism embodies the worst form of globalization advocated by those who are horrified by this phenomenon. After all, globalization supposedly projects the existence of one big world culture with many local variations, while multiculturalism proposes the creation of many "different" cultures which are actually mere mirror images of each other in that they each have the same mix of "diversity."

If all Western countries are all going to be equal mixes of African, Asian, European, Middle Eastern ways, there would be no real differences among them. The variety of the past would be suppressed and several hundred existing national and sub-national cultures would be dissolved into one basic mixture repeated endlessly, each with roughly the same proportions of Chinese, African, and other ingredients.

Of course, though this point is never explicitly considered, the advocates of this system do not intend to see them applied to Third World countries which would remain unchanged in this respect. China and Saudi Arabia, for example, would still retain distinctive traditional identities. Only Western societies would lose theirs. And here is another gigantic irony: multiculturalists who say they reject any idea that Western civilization is superior are actually implicitly claiming that it will be better than these "backward" traditionally monoculturally national ones. Countries following this pattern would be at a higher stage than "merely" national ones like Argentina, Egypt, India or China. After all, if they have their way the countries revolutionized by radical multiculturalism would embody the ultimate and superior "good" of diversity based on having no central culture but merely being a collection of them. Yet what if multiculturalism turns out well, an outcome in which immigrants are acculturated in the public sphere but can still keep some distinctiveness in their private lives while living under a single law that applies to everyone? In other words, what if multiculturalism means that the historic dominant culture remains in place however supplemented by other cultures from immigrant groups? Let's call this moderate multiculturalism as merely another name for democratic pluralism.

If this is what is going to happen the result would be another, though happier, irony. For then all these newly improved, historically monocultural countries would look increasingly like a role model they profess to dislike, the original mixing bowl nation where democratic pluralism reigns: the United States of America. Think about that: universal multiculturalism, more than globalization, would produce variant-flavored knock-offs of what the designer-original America has done with its immigrants.

In effect, this is what Rowling has done for her version of Britain. Literature, of course, has many values, including promoting the readers' happiness, understanding, and education. A great literary work contains truths about people, life, and society. So is it with the Harry Potter series. Oh, and by the way, great literary works are almost always based on a great cultural identity and tradition. Sometimes, among the best interpreters are immigrants and minority groups who have an original perspective on that society. But this is only true if they in the main accept its rules and ideas.

That is one more reason why what might be called national democratic pluralism (and Western civilization in general) is so worth preserving against the Lord—and Ayatollah—Voldemorts of the world and their little helpers.

The Politics of Harry Potter Are Not Progressive

Dana Goldstein

Dana Goldstein is a staff writer at the American Prospect. *She finds the politics of Harry Potter to be complex. Readers are meant to see the evil in Voldemort's attempt to purge the magical world of those lacking pure blood lines. Goldstein argues that racism and sexism also exist elsewhere in the novels. To support her thesis she points to the servility of the house-elves and the traditional roles of women in the books.*

What are the politics of Harry Potter? The rift in the magical world described over the course of J.K. Rowling's epic pits the young wizard and his companions against the terrorizing, fascistic Lord Voldemort, who seeks to "cleanse" the wizarding community of "mudbloods," those witches and wizards born into non-magical families. Parallels to the Holocaust and other genocides and apartheid regimes are easy to draw. Just as we're eager to hear that Hitler was part Jewish, or gay, or suffered from a terrible sexual dysfunction, Potter fans eat up the revelation that Voldemort himself had a Muggle, or non-magical, father.

Harry Potter and the Challenges of Diversity

Rowling, though famously tight-lipped, has used her personal website to draw explicit comparisons between her mythological universe and 20th century history. A young reader wrote to Rowling to ask, "Why are some people in the wizarding world

Dana Goldstein, "J.K. Rowling Subtly Critiques, Yet Ultimately Hews to, a Fantasy Script Dependent on Stereotypes Culled from Real-Life Racism," The *American Prospect*, July 24, 2007. Reproduced with permission from The *American Prospect*, 11 Beacon Street, Suite 1120, Boston, MA 02108.

(e.g., Harry) called 'half-blood' even though both their parents were magical?" She responds:

> The expressions "pure-blood," "half-blood," and "Muggle-born" have been coined by people to whom these distinctions matter, and express their originators' prejudices. . . . If you think this is far-fetched, look at some of the real charts the Nazis used to show what constituted "Aryan" or "Jewish" blood. I saw one in the Holocaust Museum in Washington when I had already devised the "pure-blood," "half-blood," and "Muggle-born" definitions and was chilled to see that the Nazis used precisely the same warped logic as the Death Eaters. A single Jewish grandparent "polluted" the blood, according to their propaganda.

Rowling describes her surprise at learning her own fictional creation mirrors historical reality. Whether we believe this stance or understand it as a pose for the benefit of young readers, Rowling clearly intends her audience to see the moral predicaments in her novels not as "far-fetched," but as quite relevant to a troubled world.

Thus, some critics have been tempted to read Harry Potter as a commentary on the 21st-century struggle to contain global terrorism. But Rowling began plotting the series in the early 1990s, and four of the seven books were written and published before the attacks of Sept. 11, 2001. The series, therefore, is less a critique of Guantanamo Bay or Abu Ghraib (echoes of which many readers see in the Ministry of Magic's cruel Azkaban prison) than a meditation on the challenge of diversity, that conundrum at the center of modern societies.

But Rowling's ideology cannot simply be described as anti-racist, for as strongly as she condemns racially-motivated violence, Harry Potter remains a classic work of fantasy. And fantasy is a literary genre intent, above almost all else, on the reassuring order of classification and categorization, of blood lines and inheritances.

Though we're meant to abhor Voldemort's obsession with "pure" blood lines, father-to-son inheritances are crucial to fulfilling Harry's destiny as savior of the magical community. The "Deathly Hallows" referred to in the title of the seventh book are three medieval magical objects made by pureblood brothers and thought to allow their owners to avoid death. Toward the end of the book, Harry learns he is the rightful heir to one of the hallows and can access the two others as well. So the boy wizard tasked with fighting the pureblood ideology is himself a descendent of one of the most prestigious families in magical history. The plot device is too conventional to be ironic, and fits squarely within the fantasy tradition of ascribing high-born histories to even the most humble heroes. Think of Aragorn in J.R.R. Tolkien's *Lord of the Rings*.

Hierarchy and Patriarchy Exist in Harry Potter's World

Like Tolkien, Rowling depicts a variety of magical species in addition to human wizards. Tolkien unabashedly racialized his magical beings: Tall, pale Elves spoke a beautiful Latinate tongue; little Hobbits were simple, fun-loving, loyal folk; and dark-skinned "southern" human tribes sided in battle with orcs, savage creatures no better than animals.

Rowling's world isn't all that different. A magical species called Veelas are high-born, fairy-like creatures who seduce men and possess unnatural, silvery-white beauty. Over the course of the books, the young wizards do learn to respect house elves, a species in slavery to human masters. Yet even in freedom, the elves' personalities are depicted as fundamentally servile. A rather pathetic elf named [Dobby] feels his subordination so keenly that when he fails in tasks assigned to him by Harry, he beats himself to a pulp. We're meant to feel sorry for [Dobby], but elves have no agency—they owe even their liberation movement to humans.

The position of women in the narrative fits this vision of prescribed social roles and hierarchies. Harry's heroes—his school headmaster, godfather, and various magical sporting figures—are all men. His dead mother, the Muggle-born Lily, is portrayed as the source of love and sacrifice in his life, while his late father, James, was daring, brash, and heroic. The books do strike some blows against gender stereotypes, portraying brave female warriors, a number of uncommonly cruel and violent female characters, and, of course, Harry's best friend Hermione, a heroine because of her ability to turn academic acumen into practical magical solutions. But on the whole, Rowling's wizarding society conforms to boringly conventional gender roles. Dads, like the loveable Mr. Weasley (father of red-headed sidekick Ron), go off to work while steadfast moms stay home cooking, cleaning, and rearing large families. Magical education doesn't begin until the age of 11, so witches are also tasked with full-time parenting and educational responsibilities over young children, Rowling clarified for a curious reader at her website.

The best window into how Rowling subtly critiques, yet ultimately hews to, a fantasy script dependent on stereotypes culled from real-life racism is the acrimony between humans and goblins, an important plot device in book seven. Goblins in the series are humanoid beings (they can mate with people) skilled at forging metal and protecting valuables. Harry and Ron distrust goblins, but the naïve Hermione reminds them that wizards have been cruel to goblins throughout history, provoking bad behavior from the creatures. Against his better instincts, Harry cuts a deal with the goblin Griphook: In exchange for help in obtaining a magical object deep with a protected vault, Harry will give Griphook a valuable medieval sword he has inherited. But Harry soon learns goblin ideas of ownership are different than human ideas; while people believe they own an object once they pay for it and can pass it to whomever they like, goblins believe a valuable object must be returned to its creator—often a goblin—upon its purchaser's death. Thus, Griphook steals the sword from Harry without fully upholding his end of the bargain. The ultimate judgment is that whole categories of creatures, even those whose blood is intermingled in the human race, cannot be trusted.

Of course, one could make the argument that Rowling is "color-blind;" her minor characters sport a variety of ethnic names—Anthony Goldstein, Parvati Patil, Cho Chang. But even as Rowling attempts to neutralize race by presenting a diverse cast of young wizards, she creates a world in which some beings are born into stereotypes they cannot overcome and that render them inherently inferior. This is, unfortunately, par for the course in the fantasy genre, in which pretend humanoid species have too often been used as a cover for our reactionary assumptions about different types of real people.

The hierarchical, patriarchal undertones of the fantasy genre will likely be lost on children caught up in Harry's quest to defeat the evil Lord Voldemort. The series is great fun, and I wouldn't deny anyone the pleasure of reading these books. But the politics of Harry Potter, while broadly anti-authoritarian, are far more complicated at the level of individual identity, and cannot be described as progressive. Perhaps this is why science fiction is ultimately a more radical genre than fantasy. While fantasy looks backwards for its myths and mores, sci-fi looks forward. So here's hoping the next J.K. Rowling washes her hands of Tolkien and, perhaps in her next series of books, popularizes Madeline L'Engle instead.

The Harry Potter Books Take a Complex View of Race

Andrew Blake

The social world of Harry Potter is more complex than it appears on the surface, Andrew Blake contends. On the one hand, the books clearly denounce the fascist pure-bloodline beliefs of Voldemort and his supporters and depict a Hogwarts that is diverse ethnically and socioeconomically. On the other hand, Blake points out, wizards are clearly superior to Muggles, and giants and house-elves are presented as inferior species. Blake is associate dean of the School of Social Sciences, Media, and Cultural Studies at the University of East London. He frequently writes reviews for the Independent *and is the author of numerous books, including* Salman Rushdie: A Beginner's Guide.

For the liberal reader the question of race and culture looks—at first sight—to be the [Harry Potter] books' strongest political suit. The books systematically deny the explicitly racist theories of bloodline held by many witches and wizards. Both Hermione's parents are from the Muggle world. People like her are welcomed into the fold by many other wizards and witches, partly because of the renewal they bring to the existing wizarding stock. Others are less positive. The aristocratic Malfoys, for example, believe that those wizards or witches who have married Muggles will produce racially impure children, 'mudbloods' as they call them. So Hermione is according to these conservative members of the wizarding world a 'mudblood'—and unwelcome. 'Wizard blood is counting for less year by year,' complains shopkeeper Mr Borgin early in *Chamber of Secrets*, while talking to Lucius Malfoy. A few pages later Hagrid reverses the implication, referring to

Andrew Blake, *The Irresistible Rise of Harry Potter*. London, UK: Verso, 2002.

the Malfoys as 'bad blood'; later he explains that the term 'mudblood' is highly controversial, and is seen as an insult. At the start of *Goblet of Fire*, in the aftermath of the Quidditch World Cup final, Voldemort's former supporters and servants—the Death Eaters—hunt for and torture any mudbloods or Muggles they can find, exactly as if they were football hooligans led by racists such as the British National Party. The Potter books may be morally ambivalent, but the magic racists are consistently represented as evil.

The Harry Potter Books Overtly Condemn Racism

In some ways Harry's own status reinforces the books' condemnation of racism. Harry Potter's wizardly lineage is part of the overall narrative of the series, and all the books so far explore aspects of his relationship with his dead parents. Harry's mother, while a witch herself, was not of 'pure' wizard lineage—her parents were not magical. We are informed in *Chamber of Secrets* that the wizardly obsession with lineage is down to Salazar Slytherin, one of the four founders of Hogwarts School. He built the Chamber of Secrets, and the legend is that whatever one day emerges from it will destroy those who are not of pure blood. During the crisis the Slytherins adopt an insurance policy—the password into Slytherin House common room is changed to 'pure-blood'. Harry is not pure in this sense. Nonetheless, the fact that he can converse in Parseltongue (the language spoken by snakes) means that Harry might be Slytherin's heir—which makes him unpopular with his schoolfellows, threatened as they are by the creature from the chamber. It turns out that Voldemort considers himself to be the heir, thanks to his mother's lineage—she is a direct descendant of Salazar Slytherin, though his father was in his own words 'a foul, common Muggle' who abandoned his mother when he realised she was a witch. In other words, this Hitler-like figure is not pure-blooded himself; and in genetic terms, he's the mirror-image of Harry. 'Pure blood' is no guarantee either of wizarding ability or of any other worth, as the books repeat time and again.

Muggles Are Inferior to Wizards

So far, so ethnically correct. There are a number of caveats. Consider the pervasive peripheral presence of an inferior species, the Muggles. They can give birth to wizards (the reverse is also true—Hogwarts caretaker Argus Filch is a 'squib', a non-magician born to magic parents); doubtless this works through some set of recessive genes. Harry's own Muggle ancestry should not blind us to the ways in which Muggles are represented as different from the wizards—and that difference, let's be clear, is constituted by a lack of ability. The stories here are not ambivalent: Muggles are represented mainly through the white, lower-middle-class, suburban Middle England, and utterly ghastly Dursleys. As such they are unlikely to gain our sympathies, and they are repeatedly trashed by Harry and his friends in ways that aren't entirely dissimilar to the Death Eaters' non-witch-hunt in *Goblet of Fire* (which is clearly presented as wrong). Dudley Dursley is given a pig's tail in *Philosopher's Stone*, [published in the United States as *Sorcerer's Stone*], when Hagrid loses his temper; it has to be surgically removed. *Prisoner of Azkaban* opens with Harry's torture of Aunt Marge, who becomes a balloon (Ministry wizards restore her at the cost of her memory of the event). Dudley is the fall guy again at the start of *Goblet of Fire*, as the Weasley twins trick him into swallowing one of the Ton-Tongue Toffee sweets they are developing for their joke shop—their father eventually repairs the damage.

In these Roald Dahlesque portrayals Muggles are *disabled*; constrained by their lack to rely on technology, while hopelessly unaware of the parallel world around them. Popular etymology has already adopted 'Muggle' as a term of abuse. Joanne Rowling may have wanted merely to identify the species when using the word, but it has already become one of contempt—one reinforced by many of the books' translators, whose attempts to provide equivalent neologisms include 'babboni' in Italian—derived from *babbioni*, idiots—and 'dreutzel' in Dutch, derived from *dreutel*, clumsy. The books do their best to raise awareness of racism, and they consistently attack ideas about purity, blood and race, but at the heart of all the stories is a semi-parallel magical world whose inhabitants are superior to ordinary humans, and that's that.

Giants and House-Elves Are Inferior

There are other problems. Giants are the subject of prejudice—in *Goblet of Fire* Ron's negative attitude to giants, typical of wizards, is contrasted with the Muggle-derived tolerance of Hermione and Harry. Another group is treated with contempt throughout the wizarding world, again to Hermione's disgust. Dobby, the house-elf who we first meet in *Chamber of Secrets*, has powerful magical powers of his own. He also has an 'ugly brown face'. He and all house-elves are slaves, and they are represented as passive victims rather than rebels against their lot: Dobby cannot escape his servitude by himself, but is freed by Harry. The house-elf subplot becomes much more complex, and arguably more disturbing, in *Goblet of Fire*, when it becomes clear that house-elf psychology tends to masochism—despite Hermione's campaigns on their behalf most of them want not to be free but to obey their 'masters'. Like the Muggles, but this time despite their own magical skills, the house-elves are an inferior species.

Hogwarts Is a Multiethnic Community

But (though there are house-elves working in the kitchens, and it's worth asking where house-elves are educated, and where they get their own magical powers) Hogwarts stands for a functioning multicultural society. It's worth noting again that Hogwarts is *not* a public school [a type of school that is called a private school in the United States] in the classic sense: it is not selective on the grounds of parental class or wizarding ability. It serves the children of the whole wizarding community—including the potentially evil Slytherins—and anyone else who is seen to have the ability to benefit from the education it offers. As far as we know, though it requires uniform, textbooks and other paraphernalia, it does not charge fees. Similarly, the Hogwarts pupils themselves are not ethnically divided. Rowling gestures consistently at the multiculturalism of much of the contemporary world. The concepts 'pure blood' and 'mudblood' have nothing to do with skin colour, or nation or culture of origin. Parvati Patil is an ordinary minor character, not a comic caricature like Hurree Ramset Jam Singh in the Billy Bunter stories, who is there to be laughed at because of his eccentric use of English.

Parvati Patil isn't alone—several of the recurring minor characters among the Hogwarts pupils are named and characterised as of Irish, African-Caribbean, South Asian or Chinese descent, and in *Goblet of Fire* we meet wizards and witches from all over the world at the Quidditch World Cup and the Triwizard Tournament. These characters aren't mere passive onlookers, mentioned only in passing: the dreadlocked (that is, symbolically African-Caribbean) Lee Jordan, for example, appears regularly as the school's Quidditch commentator. The idea of pure blood is also undermined by the ways in which characters from different ethnic groups interact. Harry's first sexual and romantic stirrings are for Cho Chang—his sporting rival, the Ravenclaw Seeker. In *Goblet of Fire*, because he has been too shy to ask Cho to go to the ball as his partner before she has promised to go with someone else, he goes with Parvati Patil. Viktor Krum, meanwhile, the Bulgarian Quidditch international Seeker who enters the Triwizard Tournament as a member of Durmstrang school, begins to develop a romantic liaison with Hermione. So the pupils live in a multicultural community in which what the real world calls 'mixed-race relationships' are common.

Hogwarts Has Class Differences

Inheritance is explored at Hogwarts in another, very English, way—the stories feature class differences and snobberies. Not all the children at Hogwarts are social equals, and neither are their parents (which is one reason why this is *not* just another public school story). Many people have noticed that the school houses map on to the class system, with the worthy workers (Hufflepuff), the brave, stolidly reliable lower middle class (Gryffindor),' and the professional and intellectual middle class (Ravenclaw). At the top of the tree, on Harry's arrival, we have Slytherin, where we find wicked aristocrats, those stock baddies of the public school story. 'You'll soon find out some wizarding families are much better than others, Potter,' drawls archetypal Slytherin Draco Malfoy on his first appearance in *Philosopher's Stone*. The wizarding world as a whole is dominated by the ghostly presence of he who must not be named, Lord Voldemort. Though this is an assumed, rather than inherited, title, like Malfoy's his name seems deliberately feudal, and—again—racialised. One reviewer of *Prisoner of Azkaban* made much of these Francophone names, pointing to France as the traditional enemy of Britain. Yes; and/but such names must also be traced back to the Norman invasion of Britain in 1066, which imposed a French ruling class on the Anglo-Saxons—this is more of an internal argument about class than an external one about nation; and once again it's locally apposite—since its 1997 election New Labour, embarrassed and confused by the remaining structures of class in Britain, has been half-heartedly trying to close down the feudal system, finally, by reforming the House of Lords.

Of course the Hogwarts house system is more complex in detail than it is in outline. The Sorting Hat does not always follow the simple class map. Each house has a mix of good scholars, incompetents, good Quidditch players and social outcasts. Slytherin has Malfoy's troll-like, and very unaristocratic bodyguards Crabbe and Goyle; and while Cedric Diggory's father, defensively boasting of his son's Quidditch ability, represents the typical Hufflepuff worker, Gryffindor also has poor people, notably the Weasleys. 'I hate being poor, it's rubbish,' says Ron in *Goblet of Fire*—and while he is reminded of this poverty by Malfoy at every opportunity from their first encounter in *Philosopher's Stone* onwards, the politics of class as well as 'blood' are particularly prominent in *Goblet of Fire*, which closes with Harry's investment in the Weasley twins' small business, an investment that may well make this genteel-poor family into the new middle class. It may even make them wealthy enough to move to somewhere like Privet Drive, and live like the Dursleys—which presumably is the fate of many who belong to the brave and reliable Gryffindor. . . .

The Postcolonial World of Harry Potter

Giselle Liza Anatol

Giselle Liza Anatol argues that while Rowling attempts to embrace multiculturalism, a closer reading of her text reveals a Eurocentric bias. She finds similarities between Rowling and Rudyard Kipling in their use of serpents to conjure up fear and danger and to equate it with the state of foreignness. Although Hogwarts has a diverse student base, Anatol notes, the students of color share the same culture as the dominant Anglo society. She concludes that the atmosphere of the Harry Potter books is thus not one of diversity and integration, but rather of assimilation. Anatol is associate professor of English at the University of Kansas and the editor of the collection Reading Harry Potter: Critical Essays.

What I aim to do . . . is examine the Harry Potter novels from a postcolonial perspective. This framework does not mean to suggest, as the term *post*colonial might indicate, that colonialism is dead and gone: theories can be used to interrogate the ways that the old colonial system has found its way back into society as neocolonialism, a revived push by dominant forces to maintain or reinvigorate their positions of social and cultural privilege. Postcolonial readings attempt to "rethink, recuperate, and reconstruct racial, ethnic, and cultural others that have been repressed, misrepresented, omitted, stereotyped, and violated by the imperial West with all its institutions and strategies for dominating the non-Western" [according to Shaobo Xie]. Attributing this damage to the entire "imperial West" is a claim too broad to allow us to unravel the complexities of our current historical situation, or for us to adequately take into account Rowling's definitively non-dominant subject position as a woman and former welfare recipient. However, I hope that by engaging with children's literature in the spirit of Xie's definition, I can challenge traditional and Eurocentric ways of seeing that are both represented within the narratives and with which many of us have been trained to interpret texts.

Harry Potter Is Part of the British Adventure-Story Tradition

I begin with the question of whether Rowling simply continues in the tradition of what Martin Green in *Dreams of Adventure, Deeds of Empire* identifies as "the energizing myth" of imperialism. Popular children's literature published during the height of Britain's imperialist era "were, collectively, the story England told itself as it went to sleep at night; and . . . they charged England's will with energy to go out into the world and explore, conquer, and rule." I argue that although the Potter series attempts to embrace ideas of global equality and multiculturalism, the stories actually reveal how difficult it is for contemporary British subjects such as Rowling to extricate themselves from the ideological legacies of their ancestors.

Through children's literature, many European nations of the eighteenth, nineteenth, and twentieth centuries instilled the imperialist and colonizing values of the adult population. As Patrick Brantlinger notes: "Much imperialist discourse was . . . directed at a specifically adolescent audience, the future rulers of the world." However, the ideology of imperialism, colonialism, and xenophobia is often encoded so deeply—both in the text itself and in our own perception of the world—that it becomes almost invisible. Rowling's novels seem particularly influenced by the British adventure story tradition, which promoted "civilized" values—resourcefulness, wits, ingenuity, and hierarchy headed by a *legitimate* democratic authority—and demonstrated their desirability in the wild territories beyond England's borders. Because imperialists often condemned the indigenous peoples of Africa, India, and the Americas as wasteful of the incredible natural resources that lay around them, in imperialist literature, the empire and its agents are typically depicted as best for everyone concerned. In other words, when all behave according to the plan, the colonials gain the majority of capital but can be reassured that the indigenous peoples have had "their standard of living raised somewhat, and their moral natures raised quite a lot" [according to M. Daphne Kutzer]. . . .

And so how do the Harry Potter novels fit into this tradition? Harry's option of staying at home with the Dursleys is obviously a dire one. . . . [It] is easy to interpret Harry's journey into the wizarding world as one into a thrilling and promising foreign space, separate from the metropole of Muggle England. Hogwarts and the surrounding magical community are a territory where the natives might be technologically primitive, but they are morally enlightened, friendly, respected and respectful, and powerful in many ways. As Kutzer notes of many fantasy works, authors expend a great deal of energy providing the specifics of local flora, fauna, native customs, and behavior. "There is a kind of ethnographic gloss to these books that suggests to the reader that foreign lands are not made-up fantasy lands, but real places that can provide real adventures, if only one can get to them." Accordingly, Harry spends a great deal of time in the wizarding world learning about new plants and creatures, such as mandrakes, hippogriffs, and unicorns, and unfamiliar practices and customs—from the Sorting Hat procedure to how to send mail by Owl Post, travel by Floo powder, and de-gnome a garden.

Beneath this aspect of foreignness, however, lies the fact that the excursions to Hogwarts are not *away* from the homeland and *to* a symbolic colonial outpost, but rather journeys back to Harry's true homespace. In the wizarding world he finds acceptance among people of his own magical kind. As he reaches his dormitory room on the first night back at school for his third year, he feels as if he is "home at last." Thus, on one hand Rowling depicts Hogwarts and its environs as a space of difference, inhabited by the Other, and quite separate from the "real" and flawed British sphere; on the other hand, however, this sphere also serves as an accurate reflection of British reality. Because the wizarding world overlaps and intersects with the Muggle world, Harry is allowed to remain in the very heart of Britain as he supposedly travels to a foreign space, discovers himself, and is initiated into adulthood. British cultural centrism and isolationism are effectively maintained.

Comparisons with Rudyard Kipling

Rudyard Kipling's fiction provides an interesting point of comparison with Rowling's series. Both writers seem trapped as they attempt to negotiate the space between longings for empire and a recognition of its potential for destruction. The novel *Kim* (1901), for example, celebrates life in India, and the diversity of people, wildlife, and landscapes of the region, but it simultaneously praises the young protagonist's induction into the British secret service—a collaboration that helps the British to rule India. Rowling appears to experience the same wavering desires between nostalgia for and opposition to neocolonial attitudes. When the Muggle groundskeeper at the Quidditch World Cup campsite suspiciously asks Mr. Weasley if he is "foreign" and remarks that the grounds have been overrun, he gives voice to a conservative anti-immigrant sentiment that Rowling overtly writes against. The divergent attitudes of Ron and Hagrid and Harry and Hermione emphasize this point. Hagrid claims that the less one has do with foreigners, the happier one will be—"Yeh can' trust any of 'em"—and Ron refuses to try the unfamiliar bouillabaisse at the Tournament welcome dinner. In contrast, Harry responds to Hagrid that [the Bulgarian student] Viktor Krum is "all right!," and Hermione not only enjoys the French dish but develops a romantic relationship with Krum as well. Together, Harry and Hermione suggest that although the wizarding world can be more insular than the Muggle world in some ways, as the "next generation" of wizards and witches, they will encourage more tolerance and an international outlook.

This tolerance, however, seems linked to the rather banal versions of "multiculturalism" that plague certain late twentieth-/early twenty-first-century communities: visions of "open-mindedness" to the Other function primarily on the level of the enjoyment and consumption of particular goods these foreigners have to offer, such as foods, film, music, and clothing. In spite of the progress that Rowling's narrative ostensibly offers, it can be observed that the underlying discourse of her work supports many of the very ideas she tries to counter. Thus, although she inverts traditional binaries and blurs the lines between domestic and foreign, civilized and savage, because the magical world is located within Britain's borders, the true center of intellectual, spiritual, and cultural enlightenment is not shifted out of the British realm.

Kipling's *The Jungle Books* (1894–1895) provide ground for further comparison between the two authors sentimentality for certain aspects of imperialist ideology. Many of the stories in Kipling's collection center on themes of invasion. In "Rikki-tikki-tavi," for example, the cobras despise the British colonial family that has moved into the bungalow because the humans threaten the snakes' dominion and the certainty that the snakes' offspring will grow up healthy, strong, and in control. The reptilian antagonists plot for the time when "the garden will be our own again." Representative of India's brown-skinned indigenous peoples, the black snakes are cast as evil, vicious, and dangerous, needing to be exterminated so that the white British colonizers can live peacefully in the land they have appropriated. . . .

Rowling Evokes Exotic Images of India

Rather than perpetuating traditional Christian concepts of serpents as evil, Rowling at first appears to contest Eurocentric norms. Hogwarts students initially shun Harry for being a Parselmouth. In *Harry Potter and the Goblet of Fire* newspaper reporter Rita Skeeter's twisted article about the "disturbed" Harry Potter quotes a member of the Dark Force Defense League, who intimates that others should be "highly suspicious" of anyone who can talk to snakes—creatures embodying the worst forces of Dark Magic and possessing a historical association with "evildoers." Minister of Magic Cornelius Fudge later reiterates the sentiment when he calls Harry's trustworthiness into question specifically because the young wizard can converse with serpents. Rowling suggests here the irony of their bigotry. In the same way that witches are ostracized in the Muggle world for having the rare gift of being able to perform magic, members of wizarding society censure Harry for his linguistic gift. Rowling's critique is clear in that Fudge is both prejudiced and a political coward, and Skeeter is detestably unethical. Harry, able to speak Parseltongue, has a link to the natural world, and, despite a demonstration of the ingenuity and resourcefulness highly regarded in early imperialist adventure stories, he chooses to employ this connection to commune with nature rather than to control and exploit it.

At the same time, however, Rowling relies on the discourse of imperialism in her use of snakes in the narrative. The word "Parseltongue" closely resembles the word "Parsee," the name of a religious community in India concentrated in Bombay. For British readers, references to Parsees might unconsciously evoke images of fakirs and other mystics who perform feats of magic or endurance, such as charming snakes from baskets and walking on coals. As Kutzer notes, the political and cultural lives of India, the "jewel in the crown" of the British Empire, and England have been inextricably entwined since the end of the nineteenth century: "Indian words had become English words: jodhpurs, verandahs, pukka, and so forth." I would therefore assert that Rowling depends upon the reader's assumption of the exotic qualities of India—romantic associations with palm readers, snake charmers, and the like—to connect snakes to fear, particularly fear of the foreign. Just as the cobra antagonists in Kipling's "Rikki-tikki-tavi" are "highly emblematic of India itself. . . . Visual shorthand for the Orient,'" snakes in the Potter books symbolize inherent femaleness, seductiveness, duplicity, sensual excess, skulking silence, and, above all, danger. Victims of the basilisk in *Harry Potter and the Chamber of Secrets* can be killed by the serpent's stare; in *Goblet of Fire*, Voldemort must milk the female snake Nagini to build up his strength and malevolent powers. Voldemort himself possesses a flat, snakelike face, replete with red gleaming eyes before his transformation, and afterwards, a ghostly white visage with a nose as "flat as a snake's" with slits for nostrils. Furthermore, Voldemort is strengthened by a ceremony that casts him as an anti-Christ—the "son" the "master" revived, and the foe "resurrected"; the end of the chapter ominously states that "*Lord* Voldemort had *risen again*"—effectively reinforcing traditional connections between snakes and Satan.

The anxiety over foreign invasion, far from being dispelled by a narrative that embraces difference, predominates in the Potter books. Danger typically comes from outside national borders. In *Harry Potter and the Sorcerer's Stone*, the three-headed dog, Fluffy, comes from a Greek, in *Chamber of Secrets*, Aragog the giant spider informs Harry and Ron that he, too, arrived from a distant territory. Hagrid found Aragog a mate and their family has grown exponentially in the Forbidden Forest, waiting for the human flesh on which they prey. The fear of immigrant entry, reproduction, and take-over seems evident in this subplot. Wizards and witches constantly worry about the threat of Muggles discovering and invading the magical realm; the antagonism against Muggle-borns

The three stars of the Harry Potter films, Rupert Grint, Emma Watson, and Daniel Radcliffe (from left to right). Although Rowling attempts to make the Harry Potter series multicultural, the main characters are Eurocentric. AP Images.

stems, in part, from a distrust of their motives after years of persecution at the hands of the nonmagical. . . .

[Rather] than functioning as symbolic of the colonial territory, the school of magic comes to symbolize the imperial center that unenlightened foreigners threaten to infiltrate, leading to the obliteration of its people. Is it significant that Voldemort and his forces, like Kipling's black snakes, are portrayed in terms of darkness, and to be "dark" is to be evil? Perhaps not. However, the ancient castle clearly stands as a beacon of safety for the side of good, and represents the longevity and stability of Britain's history and civilization. . . .

Harry first encounters the merpeople during the Triwizard Tournament of book IV. This event, which serves as the framework for *Goblet of Fire*, is described as a seven-hundred-year-old tradition, established as a friendly competition between the three largest schools of magic. Its purpose is to lay the foundation of relationships between young wizards and witches of various nationalities. While the message of international camaraderie and cooperation is a positive one and emphasized throughout the story, it is quite noticeable that none of the schools represented comes from outside of the Eurasian continent. . . . Rowling novels do little to alter the Western notion that "outlying regions of the world have no life, history, or culture to speak of, no independence or integrity worth representing without the West" [according to Edward W. Said]. . . .

Hogwarts Promotes International Goodwill

Hogwarts's position on the ethical high ground, with its students and teachers of superior character, shines through . . . when Dumbledore invites all of the foreign pupils back to Hogwarts at any time they wish to visit. He urges bonds of friendship and trust in order to successfully defeat Voldemort: cultural and linguistic differences are "nothing at all if our aims are identical and our hearts are open." The British school promotes international goodwill, the inspiration for the battle against evil, and stands as the emblem of enlightened thought.

The obvious question: what would the result of this policy of open borders be? Amongst conventional children's adventure stories, non-European cultures are established as the inferior Other, and non-white, non-European characters who are central to the plots are either well-assimilated into the mainstream or comic in their attempts to blend in. The position of the students of color in their Hogwarts surroundings is therefore telling as to Rowling's conception of multiculturalism. While most discussions of race and racism in the novels operate on a symbolic level, analyzing Rowling's representation of metaphorical Others in the human wizarding world, including Muggle-borns, giants, trolls, and house-elves, I would like to explore the depiction of literal Otherness in the predominantly white, British environs of Hogwarts.

Cho Chang, the Patil twins, Dean Thomas, Lee Jordan, and Angelina Johnson reveal that a diversity of races and ethnicities are represented at Harry Potter's school. Cho Chang's name suggests that she is Chinese; Parvati and Padma Patil's names similarly point to South Asian identity. During the first-year sorting, Dean is described as "a Black boy even taller than Ron," and while not a definitive racial marker, Lee Jordan's dreadlocks hint at possible African-Jamaican ancestry. In *Goblet of Fire*, Rowling describes Angelina as the "tall black girl" who plays one of the Chasers on Gryffindor's Quidditch team.

Noticeably, however, the inclusion of people of color does not mean the inclusion of any representation of ethnic difference and cultural practices. Parvati's and Cho's ethnicities are evident in their names, but *only* in their names. And while all of the students mentioned might be visually apparent to the characters within the fictional storyline, their visual difference for the reader quickly disappears and their racial identities fade into the background. In a world where white people are the dominant social group, whiteness becomes the "default" for unmentioned race; it is interpreted as the norm and assumed when unstated. Rowling thus finds herself in an ideological bind—while she perhaps attempts to display a "colorblind" society where everyone is distinguished solely by magical ability, she makes it supremely easy for the reader to forget (or ignore) the multiethnic surroundings that she initially seeks to establish. . . .

Students of Color Are Assimilated, Not Integrated

Rowling makes a strong move towards encouraging multiculturalism, especially with her messages condemning the bigotry of both normative Muggles like the Dursleys, pure-blood witches and wizards who scorn "Mudbloods," and all magical folk who assume the natural inferiority of house-elves and fear and persecute giants and werewolves. On a more literal level Hogwarts enrolls several students of color, who are mentioned numerous times throughout the books, and many of the couples at the Yule Ball during Harry's fourth year at Hogwarts are interracial—Cedric and Cho, Fred and Angelina, Ron and Padma, and Harry and Parvati. All suggest the integration of people of various races at the school and the hope for tolerance among people of the larger magical community. At the same time, however, Rowling undermines this reading; to date, the novels portray not integration and acceptance, but the complete assimilation of Dean, Lee, Angelina, Parvati, Padma, and Cho into the all-white landscape of Hogwarts students and teachers. In stressing a liberal humanist message of "we are all the same beneath the surface" and asserting that race and ethnicity *should* not be important in judging another person, Rowling's text conveys the message that race and ethnicity *are* not important for those who experience life from this position—hardly true of late twentieth/early twenty-first century Britain, Canada, the United States, or much of the rest of the world.

One possibility for why racial identity *cannot* be mentioned in Rowling's texts is that the works wobble between seeking a way out of the imperialist agenda and experiencing a certain nostalgia for the safety and security attributed to the empire. In order to perpetuate the notion that her characters of color are "true Brits" and belong to the national landscape, they must symbolically disappear from this landscape—visually, if not physically. My concern lies in how this translates for young readers: just beneath the surface, the novels propose that in order to be accepted, popular, and successful, one's differences must be ignored. And, although the *existence* of differences may be a reality, acknowledging these differences is taboo. . . .

The literature of most anglophone, or English-speaking, countries has been strongly influenced by the British

Empire. . . . In our current era of so-called globalization, it is interesting to note that while approximately 70 percent of children's books in France have been translated into French from other languages—predominantly English—less than 1 percent of books published in English are translations. British (and U.S.) texts still dominate the market throughout the English-speaking Caribbean and Africa as well. All of these figures have tremendous implications for the cultural, political, and social ideas that get spread throughout the world. Because literature can so readily be wielded as a weapon of assimilation, we must understand the imperialist ideology encoded within—especially when it is ensconced in the discourse of postcolonial resistance, proposing to support the position of the minority—and contest it within our daily lives.

Reactions to Harry Potter Reflect Global Differences and Similarities

Daniel Nexon

The extraordinary worldwide success of the Harry Potter books is both a product of and a contributor to cultural globalization, states Daniel Nexon. The books have inspired admiration and sparked controversy around the world. Nexon notes that reactions to the series in a particular country are likely to be shaped by the events and culture of that country. While different countries may vary in their interpretations of the books, Nexon argues, readers around the world have noted the similarities in J.K. Rowling's books to real-life political issues such as terrorism, civil liberties, and racial politics. Nexon is an assistant professor in the department of government at Georgetown University.

As a franchise, "Harry Potter" thrills its fans, annoys some prominent literary critics and generates large sums of money for its author and corporate backers. And its evolution holds any number of lessons for publishers, marketing executives, and other members of the industrial-entertainment complex. But in the course of its spectacular rise, "Harry Potter" has become more than simply a commercial success story: It has become a global phenomenon.

Harry Potter as an International Rorschach Test

"Harry Potter," in fact, functions something like a Rorschach Blot [a personality evaluation test involving a series of inkblots interpreted by the subject]: In countries around the

Daniel Nexon, "'Harry Potter' and Magical Realism," The *New Republic*, July 20, 2007. Reproduced by permission of The *New Republic*.

world, it captures various national anxieties about contemporary culture and international affairs. French intellectuals, for example, debate whether or not "Harry Potter" indoctrinates youngsters into the orthodoxy of unfettered market capitalism. Some Swedish commentators decry what they perceive as "Harry Potter's" Anglo-American vision of bourgeoisie conformity and its affirmation of class and gender inequality. In Turkey, we find a significant discussion of "Harry Potter" that pivots around issues of Turkish civilizational identity: whether Turkey is part of the West, the East, or a bridge between the two. A few Turkish writers have even asserted that controversies over "Harry Potter" in the United States demonstrate how Turks are more "Western" than Americans. And in Russia, a country whose concern over international status and prestige becomes more apparent each day, the newspaper *Novaya Gazeta* created a minor firestorm when it claimed that the film visage of Dobby the House-Elf was a deliberate insult to President Vladimir Putin.

More fundamentally, reactions to "Harry Potter" highlight the worldwide character of clashes between various forms of traditionalism and modernism. To many religious conservatives, "Harry Potter" represents yet another assault by the mass media, public institutions, and other manifestations of secular culture against their traditional values. In the United States, Russia, Thailand, and Australia, some Christian conservatives have condemned the books for, among other things, promoting occultism and Satanism. Harry Potter and his friends, after all, use magic and witchcraft, not only as part of their everyday lives, but also as part of their struggle against the forces of evil. Christian critics of "Harry Potter" argue that the Bible makes clear that all magic stems from demonic sources. By teaching children that witchcraft is acceptable and by encouraging them to play with wands and cauldrons, Harry Potter risks seducing them away from Christianity and into occult practices. It may even, the argument goes, bring them into contact with the very real demons that haunt our world. According to the American Library Association, Rowling's books were the fourth most challenged library books from 1990–2004, and the most challenged from 2000–2005 [the ALA defines a challenge as a formal request to remove reading material from a library or school].

Members of other religious movements also find fault with "Harry Potter." The series is enormously popular in Indonesia, the Gulf States, and many other Islamic countries. But the Wahhabist tradition [a conservative Islamic movement], as Peter Mandaville, assistant professor of government and politics at George Mason University, and Patrick Jackson, associate professor of international relations at American University, have noted, strongly opposes "various esoteric and mystical practices that . . . entered popular Islamic practice." For Wahhabists, those who practice such "heterodox" forms of Islam amount to "magicians and witches." Thus, it comes as little surprise that some Wahhabist authorities, as well as adherents to other conservative Islamic traditions, view "Harry Potter" as promoting paganism and undermining Islam. Although the specifics of the doctrinal objections differ from their Christian counterparts, the parallels remain striking.

Cultural Globalization and Harry Potter

Moreover, the reception of the books also reveals a number of important dimensions of globalization. Americans increasingly see themselves as objects of economic globalization, whether in the form of "outsourcing" or the impact of Chinese imports on U.S. manufacturing. But we still tend to think of cultural globalization as synonymous with "Americanization." The "Harry Potter" books—with their distinctively British boarding school setting, slang, and cuisine—provide a subtle rejoinder to such impressions and subvert the equation of globalization with relentless homogenization.

In fact, "Harry Potter's" worldwide popularity owes much to the deliberate and inadvertent adaptation of the series to meet local tastes. The Chinese editions translate aspects of the western folklore in "Harry Potter" into Chinese mythological traditions. Translators of the books wrestle—often unsuccessfully—with how to convert faithfully Rowling's extensive use of puns and idioms into other languages. Unauthorized "sequels" in China and India explicitly recast "Harry Potter" in local settings and using local plot devices. (In the Indian fake novel, for example, he makes friends with a Bengali boy and tours India.) Fans produce a worldwide stream of fiction set in the Harry Potter universe, each extending elements of the novels to reflect their own interests and preferences. For all its often crass commercialization, "Harry Potter's" success owes something to a process of hybridization familiar to scholars of cultural globalization.

The "Harry Potter" books lend themselves well to real-world political debates, because their plots themselves intersect with a surprising number of themes in real-world politics. The evil Voldemort and his Death Eaters, both in their organization and tactics, bear a striking resemblance to transnational terrorists. Their hatred of the impure—particularly those "mudbloods" who, despite their magical powers, lack wizarding parentage—and thirst for power genuflects in the direction of fascism, whether of the traditional or, as some might see it, the "Islamo-" variety. The Death Eaters, at least in the first six books, hide among the general wizarding population and strike with relative impunity against an often hapless Ministry of Magic with its bumbling bureaucrats and politicians. The former Minister of Magic, Cornelius Fudge, spends the last years of his tenure denying and downplaying the Death-Eater threat. "Harry Potter" heroes fight back by forming their own clandestine organization—the Order of the Phoenix—and, when necessary, bending the rule of law as they seek to defeat Voldemort's bid for global mastery.

A man skims a Persian translation of the latest Harry Potter book in Tehran, Iran, which shows the global success of the Harry Potter series. AP Images.

Harry Potter, however, is no Jack Bauer [the TV series *24*'s protagonist, a counterterrorism agent who uses torture as an interrogation method]. For those concerned about sacrificing civil liberties and democratic values to the war on terrorism, Rowling has much to offer. Innocents frequently find themselves imprisoned in the dreadful dungeon of Azkaban, which some might read as the Potterverse's own version of Guantanamo Bay. A wide variety of miscarriages of justice mark the novels. Albus Dumbledore, the moral center of the first six books, often deplores the excesses of the Ministry during the first and second struggle against the Death Eaters. He also condemns the legal inequalities that permeate the wizarding world.

Multiculturalism in Harry Potter

The books tackle not only issues of inequality, but also of multiculturalism. Class antagonism, prejudice against mudbloods, and intolerance of non-human species abound in Hogwarts and the broader wizarding community. Rowling's witches and wizards, however, display almost total indifference to Muggle racial categories. Rowling strives mightily to present a consistent moral vision of equality, but as critics such as Debra Thompson, a doctoral candidate in political science at the University of Toronto, note, she often seems to inadvertently endorse essentialist notions of racial differences. Such tensions, of course, are also endemic in real-world manifestations of multiculturalism and racial politics.

Such themes reflect, at least in part, what we might term the "partially globalized" character of "Harry Potter's" world. Divisions of the Ministry of Magic concern themselves with regulating imports. The Ministry, for example, standardizes cauldron thickness to prevent dangerous and inferior goods from flooding the market. International bodies and legal regimes govern aspects of wizard behavior. The Quidditch World Championship parallels Soccer's World Cup; it simultaneously affirms national differences while providing a focal point for cosmopolitan sporting competition. The Triwizard Tournament that forms the centerpiece of the fourth book, "Harry Potter and the Goblet of Fire," aims to establish ties "between young witches and wizards of different nationalities"—sort of like an Olympics with flying broomsticks.

At this point, however, the global "Harry Potter" phenomenon has outgrown the specifics of the books. Entrenched as they now are in the public consciousness, the characters have become symbols—abstract representations rather than the specific products of Rowling's imagination. Thus, during his 2002 election campaign, for example, Dutch Prime Minister Jan Peter Balkenende proudly embraced comparisons between himself and Daniel Radcliffe's Harry Potter to help promote his image as, according to Agence France Presse, "reliable and upright but not stuffy." But, when the Belgian Prime Minister, Guy Verhofstadt, described Balkenende as "a mix between Harry Potter and a worthy burgher, a man in whom I detect no trace of charisma," it strained relations between the two governments. Liberals in the United States, for their part, affix bumper stickers such as "Republicans for Voldemort" and "Cheney-Voldemort '08" to their cars. Voldemort may be fast on his way to becoming a general symbol for evil.

Perhaps one day, then, soon-to-be-defeated senators will justify a war not with reference to J.R.R. Tolkein's "Lord of the Rings" but to J.K. Rowling's "Harry Potter." Indeed, the world might be a better place if future politicians and Supreme Court justices look to Harry Potter, rather than "24"'s Jack Bauer, for guidance on the legitimacy of torture. But it will be a long time before we know if Rowling's creations achieve the status of global political currency. It may happen. After all, from Indonesia to Taiwan, the United States to Iran, and Russia to India, "Harry Potter" is already part of the globalizing process, with all its complexities, tensions, and possibilities.

The Harry Potter Books Reflect an Increasingly Dangerous World

Nathaniel Rivers

Nathaniel Rivers argues that the world of Harry Potter is growing increasingly darker as the series progresses, reflecting a real world made scarier by terrorism. Rivers finds numerous parallels to terrorism and reactions against terrorism in Harry Potter and the Half-Blood Prince. *He contends that the value of the book is as "an emotional survival guide" that permits children to experience scary events, where danger comes unexpectedly, but where safety is ultimately upheld. Rivers is a PhD candidate and graduate instructor at Purdue University.*

Of all the possible ways terrorism can impact a population, the psychological ones are the most often forgotten, and the most forgotten population in terms of psychological impacts are the young. This fact was never clearer to me than it was while reading the sixth and latest installment of the J.K. Rowling's Harry Potter series, *Harry Potter and the Half-Blood Prince.*

The World Has Become More Dangerous for Children

It will perhaps be noted that the books have grown progressively darker. This is due, in part, to Rowling's response to a fan base grown more mature since *Harry Potter and the Sorcerer's Stone*. It is also due, it seems, to the darkening horizon for children who read them. Acknowledging the fact that there are many children living in places where acts of terror

Nathaniel Rivers, "Harry Potter and the Half-Blood Prince," *Sycamore Review: Literature, Opinion, and the Arts*, January 15, 2008. Reproduced by permission.

are an everyday occurrence, safety is still largely taken for granted in the United States (where a third of all Harry Potter novels are sold), and, barring the sporadic terrorist acts of the Irish Republican Army, it is expected in Great Britain (the real home of the fictional Potter) as well. 9/11 was an altogether new and frightening experience for the readership of Harry Potter (the July [2005] terror attacks in London occurred just weeks before the release of the *Half-Blood Prince*). At times, our response to terrorism has been equally terrifying for young children.

My sister, Katherine, a huge Harry Potter fan, was only ten when she was frisked at our own regional airport. We now have a generation of children coming of age in a nation uneasy and unsure of what to tell them about this new setting. We are, nevertheless, trying.

Terror in Harry Potter's World Mirrors Terror in the Real World

No coming of age story has been more popular in the last several years than that of Harry Potter. A whole group of children who first came to Harry at the age of eleven in 1997 have watched him grow, and have matured along with him. In *Harry Potter and the Half-Blood Prince*, Potter comes of age, literally achieving adult status in the Wizarding world, and as Harry has wisened so have the books. Each book is a little more grown up, a little darker. The latest book, to my mind, is the darkest and most grown-up yet. Indeed, the first chapter portrays a heated discussion between a fictional British Prime Minister and the Minister of Magic about the most recent acts of terror perpetrated by Lord Voldemort.

> "A grim mood has gripped the country," the opponent had concluded, barely concealing his own broad grin.
>
> And unfortunately, this was perfectly true. The Prime Minister felt it himself; people really did seem more miserable

In this scene from the Warner Brothers film Harry Potter and the Order of the Phoenix, *Daniel Radcliffe, Rupert Grint, and Emma Watson (left to right) cower in terror.* AP Images.

> than usual. Even the weather was dismal; all this chilly mist in the middle of July. . . . It wasn't right, it wasn't normal. . . .

The opening chapter is not about Harry Potter; it is about the terror in Potter's world.

I would argue that more than anything, it is about the world of its audience. The fictional account of these non-fictional feelings connects the unreal events of the book to the very real emotions of its audience in response to the equally unreal events of their world. Other connections to terrorism abound as well. For instance, the Ministry of Magic's flyer "Protecting Your Home and Family Against Dark Forces," a flyer that lists "simple security guidelines" that "will help protect you, your family, and your home from attack," eerily resembles similar documents produced by our own Department of Homeland Security. Throughout his sixth year at Hogwarts, Harry is forced to deal with the Dark Arts more directly. Adult supervision is less certain and less present and the safe environment that once sheltered Harry and the other students is daily made less safe and more susceptible to attack. Indeed, a major and climatic episode in *Half-Blood Prince* is an infiltration of the school by a small band of Dark Wizards with the help of a Dark Force within the school. Terror thus pervades all levels of the wizarding world. Based on these and other connections and the maturing themes of the books, it is my contention that value of the book for children lies in places other than the magical world of Potter.

Its value lies in its all too realistic vision of the young reader's world. In this way, much of the book can be read as an emotional survival guide that allows children and adolescents the opportunity to experience a new environment where safety no longer remains a given, but where "safety," as an ideal, is still expected. In other words, *The Half-Blood Prince* portrays a world where danger comes from unexpected places at unexpected times, where dark forces are capable of striking at the heart of a child's fragile world.

Omnivorous critic at large Kenneth Burke wrote that literature serves as equipment for living, and J.K. Rowling has produced an equipment for children growing up in a world where danger is no longer a physical challenge reserved for adults, but is also an emotional one presented to them.

Rowling Uses Terrorism to Create Fear in the Harry Potter Books

Julia Turner

Julia Turner, culture editor of Slate *magazine, finds that, following the terrorist attacks of September 11, 2001, Rowling used real events from the war on terror as a form of shorthand to instill a sense of fear in the Harry Potter series. While Voldemort was an abstract villain in the early Harry Potter novels, in* Harry Potter and the Half-Blood Prince *he assumes the role of a terrorist and becomes even more frightening. However, Turner questions whether the contemporary references will ultimately date the books, making them less timeless, and she says that Rowling may regret relying so strongly on current events.*

In *Harry Potter and the Half-Blood Prince*, Voldemort takes up terrorism. The Dark Lord and his Death Eaters—who had gained strength in the earlier installments and have finally arrived in force—use their newfound power to spread fear in familiar ways. They destroy bridges. They murder innocents. They compel children to kill their elders. (They're also behind a magical and destructive hurricane. Does J.K. Rowling know something we don't?)

Rowling Uses Terrorism to Make Her Novel Scary

The response of the wizarding world also rings a few bells. The Ministry of Magic issues pamphlets on "Protecting Your Home and Family Against Dark Forces." Fred and George Weasley's shop makes a mint selling Shield Cloaks, which pro-

Julia Turner, "When Harry Met Osama: Terrorism Comes to Hogwarts," *Slate*, July 20, 2005.

tect their wearers from harm. The new Minister of Magic jails an innocent man, hoping to stave off panic and create the impression that he's taking action. And Harry, Hermione, and Ron greet the morning paper with a familiar sense of dread: "Anyone we know dead?"

What is J.K. Rowling up to here? Is she criticizing the War on Terror or simply using it as a plot device? In some scenes, she does take jabs at the Bush and Blair administrations. The Ministry of Magic's security pamphlet, for example, recalls the much-scorned TIPS program: "Should you feel that a family member, colleague, friend or neighbor is acting in a strange manner, contact the Magical Law Enforcement Squad at once." And Harry has a telling confrontation with the Minister of Magic, who thinks that in the battle against Voldemort, perceptions matter most. "If you were to be seen popping in and out of the Ministry from time to time," he tells Harry, "that would give the right impression. . . . It would give everyone a lift to think you were more involved." Harry refuses. He doesn't want to endorse the ministry when it's sending innocent men to Azkaban—the wizard penitentiary that becomes, in this installment, a stand-in for Gitmo [the controversial Guantanamo Bay detention camp]. "It's your duty to check that people really are Death Eaters before you chuck them in prison," Harry says.

These moments elicit grim smiles of recognition and have led some bloggers to label *Harry Potter and the Half-Blood Prince* an anti-American screed. But close reading of the book suggests that Rowling's motives are more authorial than political. She's not using Harry to make points about terrorism. She's using terrorism to make points about Harry. Rowling culls the scariest elements of modern life and uses them as a kind of shorthand, a quick way to instill fear.

In many ways, this strategy makes sense. *Half-Blood Prince* is 200 pages shorter than the installment that preceded it, in part because Rowling does not spend as much time inventing bogeymen and describing how they frighten us. Instead she uses small touches here and there—the dismal tidings in *The Daily Prophet*, the escalating instances of parental panic—to evoke a fear that her readers have already felt. This new approach is powerful. In 1998, when the first Harry Potter book came out, Voldemort was a fantastical villain, a symbol of evil in the abstract. Today, however, as we substitute for our abstract fear of Voldemort the very real fear we've felt in our own immolated cities, the new book resonates in ways that the old ones have not.

Use of Current Events May Make Books Dated

It is hard not to wonder, though, whether making the books more timely will make them less timeless. Critics have been atwitter about Harry Potter lately. Some believe the books belong alongside the classics of children's literature. Others scoff that Hogwarts is no Narnia—that the world Rowling has imagined is narrowly conceived and filled with too many cheap references to our own. Reading the *Half-Blood Prince* today, Rowling's references to terrorism don't feel cheap. They feel terrifying. But how will they read in 50 years?

In the long run, Rowling may wish she hadn't relied so much on current events. Because the book plays on a very particular set of fears, it may begin to seem dated as time goes by. Which is a shame, because Rowling is more than capable of creating enduring villains. Her best are the soul-sucking dementors that first appear in *The Prisoner of Azkaban*. These ghouls are vividly drawn and very scary. "Get too near a dementor," she writes, "and every good feeling, every happy memory will be sucked out of you. . . . You will be left with nothing but the worst experiences of your life." With the dementor, Rowling managed to make a convincing thug out of depression itself. It is inspired creations like these that win readers over and make books last.

Rowling Critiques Britain's Handling of the War on Terror

Judith Rauhofer

Judith Rauhofer, a research fellow in Law, Information, and Converging Technologies at the University of Central Lancashire, finds parallels between the actions of the Ministry of Magic in the Harry Potter series and counterterrorism measures put into place by the British government since the terrorist attacks of September 11, 2001. She contends that Rowling draws these parallels to point out the threats to civil liberties created by changes in surveillance, detention, identity cards, and security plans.

Rowling's talent for providing us with accurate and to the point political and social commentary on the public's state of mind, our day-to-day concerns and our relationship with our political leaders surely contributes to the [Harry Potter series'] appeal. She infuses the books with wit and irony, creating a subtext within the narrative which is almost exclusively accessible to adults. If parody as a literary concept is the imitation of another author's style which one wishes to expose or ridicule, in a social or political context, Rowling's description of an alternative society, its members and its government exposes and often ridicules recent events in contemporary society. In her writing she reveals situations, political wrangling, power-play and the values of a confused and morally exhausted electorate. Cultural studies expert Jeremy Gilbert observed early on in the series that "the books can be read as both commentary and exemplification of the distinct political

Judith Rauhofer, "Defence Against the Dark Arts: How the British Response to the Terrorist Threat Is Parodied in J.K. Rowling's *Harry Potter and the Half-Blood Prince*," *International Journal of Liability and Scientific Enquiry*, vol. 1, 2007, pp. 95, 96, 98–108.

moment of Tony Blair's core aspiration"; the parallel society in which the stories are set portraying Blairite values such as 'multi-culturism' and 'individual liberalism'. As the UK's love affair with the New Labour government comes to an end, so the relationship between the wizarding community and its equivalent, the 'Ministry of Magic', deteriorates, when Harry and his friends begin to take a much more critical attitude to the activities of the 'Department for Magical Law Enforcement', the 'aurors' and the 'unspeakables'. In the two books written by Rowling since the terrorist attacks in New York, Washington and Pennsylvania on 11 September 2001, the 'political thread' going through the series largely focuses on the way in which the Ministry of Magic deals with the obvious threat of Lord Voldemort's return [as written by J. Taylor]:

> [Lord Voldemort's band of followers], the Death Eaters are hard to identify, see, because they live among regular everyday wizards and only make themselves known during occasional spectacular acts of violence, which occur without warning and harm innocent people. . . . The Ministry of Magic, though working overtime to catch the real Death Eaters, is also preoccupied with saving face; they issue inane lists of precautionary steps citizens can take to protect themselves, they try to court Harry Potter . . . as a celebrity endorsement for their program, and they occasionally arrest innocent people to appear as if they're accomplishing something.

Rowling traces the British post-9/11 experience, paranoia and panic of both the general public and the ruling class succinctly and with an unfailing instinct for the peculiar. This paper will look at the various aspects of Rowling's treatment of the executive response to the terrorist threat and draw parallels between Rowling's depiction of anti-Voldemort security measures in the Potter books and the legal and political developments in the area of counter-terrorism in the UK since 2001. It will examine the way in which anti-terrorist measures adopted by the British government are in conflict with many of the values it purported to espouse when it first came to power and how the frequent departure from these values in the context of the proclaimed 'war on terror' is portrayed and subtly criticised by Rowling in her last two books.

Surveillance and Interception of Communication

> 'And lastly, while you stay here, The Burrow has been given the highest security the Ministry of Magic can provide. These measures have caused a certain amount of inconvenience to Arthur and Molly—all their post, for instance, is being searched at the Ministry, before being sent on. They do not mind in the slightest for their only concern is your safety.' [*Harry Potter and the Half-Blood Prince*]

Rowling first portrays the use of surveillance and the interception of communications in the context of a conflict between her main protagonist and the Ministry of Magic in "The Order of the Phoenix". The Ministry, concerned that Harry's account of the rebirth of his old adversary, Lord Voldemort, might worry the wizarding community, tries to contain this information. A 'High Inquisitor' is appointed to oversee the running of Hogwarts, the wizarding school Harry and his friends attend, and very soon measures are put into place to ensure both that the Ministry is aware of any communication Harry might receive from the outside world and that such communication itself is limited. Harry is told that 'all channels of communication in and out of [Hogwarts] are being monitored'. This includes the monitoring of the floo network—a wizarding communication and transportation device operating through the interconnection of wizards' fireplaces—as well as the interception of normal mail. It is likely that the Inquisitor's interception authority, like most of her other powers, is based on a ministerial 'Educational Decree', a form of executive regulatory instrument which the Ministry uses throughout the book for the purpose of imposing more and more restrictive measures on the school, its students and its teachers. Rowling's use of the Decrees highlights how the use of executive control without proper judicial oversight can lead to the suppression of dissent by those in power.

Back in the muggle world at the turn of the new millennium, the UK government also tried to improve its ability to gain information from its citizens' private communications. Certain acts of covert surveillance had already been possible under the Interception of Communications Act 1985. However, it argued that with the advent of the Internet and the increased use of e-mail, the existing powers of the police and other security services were increasingly insufficient for the prevention and prosecution of crime. Existing powers were also not always compatible with the Human Rights Act 1998 which was due to come into force in October 2000. Consequently, when a new legislative instrument was proposed in the form of the Regulation of Investigatory Powers Bill [which became the Regulation of Investigatory Powers Act, or RIPA] then Home Secretary Jack Straw presented it as merely an attempt by the government to adapt existing powers to a new legal and technological framework, claiming that "the Human Rights Act and rapidly changing technology" were the "twin drivers of the new Bill." . . .

It is not disputed that covert surveillance may be useful and has a place in the armoury of an effective police and security service. Rowling, too, has acknowledged this in "The Half-Blood Prince" when [Hogwarts headmaster] Dumbledore advises Harry that the mail of his friends, the Weasleys, will be opened and searched to ensure his safety. However, RIPA has been widely criticised as going beyond that, as starting out as a "dog's breakfast" [according to R. Cajella] and ending up as a "Snoopers Charter" which provides a "legal shield for existing mass surveillance techniques that have been ruled in breach of the European Convention [of Human Rights]" [according to R. Chandrani]. In any case, the legislation permits significant intrusion upon an individual's privacy, in secret and with very little judicial oversight.

Detention and Internment

> Stanley Shunpike, conductor of the popular wizarding conveyance the Knight Bus, has been arrested on suspicion of Death Eater activity. Mr Shunpike, 21, was taken into custody last night after a raid on his Clapham home. . . . [*Harry Potter and the Half-Blood Prince*]

While the Ministry of Magic urgently seeks to find a way in which to stem the tide of attacks suffered by both the wizarding and the muggle community, news reaches Harry that an acquaintance of his has been taken into custody after he was allegedly overheard talking about the Death Eaters' secret plans. Although neither Harry, Headmaster Albus Dumbledore nor the Ministry officials who interview him believe that Stan is guilty of any offence—Stan is described elsewhere in the books as a 'spotty youth' with a tendency to tell tall tales—he is kept in the wizard prison Azkaban for the duration of the school year. When Harry confronts the Minister for Magic with what he sees as an abuse of Ministry power, the latter replies that "these are dangerous times and certain measures need to be taken".

The detention of terrorist subjects in the UK has a long history mainly connected to its "longstanding experience concerning terrorism relating to the affairs of Northern Ireland" [as reported in *Counter-terrorism Powers: Reconciling Security and Liberty in an Open Society: a Discussion Paper*]. . . .

[In] November 2001, following the attacks on New York, Washington and Pennsylvania, the Anti-Terrorism Crime and Security Act 2001 (ATCSA) was adopted. . . . Under s. 23(1) ATCSA, a "suspected international terrorist" could be detained indefinitely where it is intended to remove or deport the person from the UK but where removal or deportation is not for the time being possible. This "inability to deport" had arisen from the ECHR [European Court of Human Rights] decisions in Soering vs. UK in 1989 and Chahal vs. UK in 1996. In both cases the applicants complained that their extradition or deportation from the United Kingdom to their respective home countries violated their rights under Art. 3 of the European Convention (freedom from torture and inhumane treatment).... As Colin Warbrick explains, this is of particular significance in the response of states to international terrorism where the government finds itself in a position where it would prefer to secure the return of a suspect to his home state rather than try him for offences, but where it is unable to do that because the suspect alleges that there is a real risk of Convention-incompatible treatment....

Identity Issues

> 4. Agree security questions with close friends and family so as to detect Death Eaters masquerading as others by use of Polyjuice Potion.... [*Harry Potter and the Half-Blood Prince*]

After Lord Voldemort's return to power, the Ministry of Magic issues a leaflet titled "Protecting your home and your family against dark forces" to all members of the wizarding community. The leaflet, which is not unlike the leaflet "Preparing for Emergencies—what you need to know", produced by the UK Government and delivered to all UK households in 2005, contains a number of security guidelines which are alleged to help protect wizards, their family and their home from attack by Lord Voldemort and his supporters. Among other things, the leaflet advises that friends and family should agree [on] 'security questions' to be able to verify each others' identity and to prevent impersonations. Most characters in the book ignore this advice, including Headmaster Albus Dumbledore, who agrees with Harry that the system seems rather pointless. After jokingly reprimanding Harry that he had not asked Dumbledore what his favourite flavour of jam was, he

Similarities can be seen between the actions of Lord Voldemort and the Ministry of Magic in the Harry Potter series and counterterrorism tactics by the British government after the 9/11 attacks. Eric Charbonneau/WireImage/Getty Images.

points out that "of course, if I were a Death Eater, I would be sure to research my own jam-preferences before impersonating myself".

Although since the 9/11 attacks many governments have focussed on identity verification as part of their counter-terrorism strategies, the UK has had a chequered history in relation to mandatory ID cards. They were last introduced under the National Registration Act 1939, a piece of wartime emergency legislation which provided for the creation of a National Register containing certain personal data of all persons living in the UK at the time. . . .

Although the wartime rationale for the Act—the need to be able to plan for manpower and the possibility of rationing—gradually fell away after the war, the cards were retained for civilian purposes. Although the subject of widespread public resentment, they were only finally discarded following the case of Willcock vs. Muckle in 1951. . . .

Since then, successive governments have attempted to reintroduce ID cards. . . .

[In] 1996 the Tory Government confirmed its intention to publish a draft Bill on the introduction of a voluntary card scheme (Select Committee on Home Affairs, 1996b). However, the calling of the May 1997 General Election prevented any further developments.

Incoming Prime Minister Tony Blair had already made it clear in his speech to the 1995 Labour conference in Brighton that he did not regard the introduction of ID cards as a priority for his new government. . . .

This attitude changed gradually after the September 11 attacks. Although originally stating that the introduction of an identity card scheme would not be part of the government's response, the then Home Secretary, David Blunkett, confirmed that the policy would be kept under review. In July 2002, the Home Office published a consultation paper followed by a summary of findings in November 2003 when [it] announced its decision to proceed with a compulsory national identity cards scheme. On 26 April 2004, the Government launched a consultation document on the legislation required for the introduction of identity cards which now also required the inclusion of 'biometric' data, that is, data such as facial dimensions, fingerprints or iris images. The scheme envisaged the use of cards, containing a certain amount of personal data and a secure encrypted chip containing a unique personal biometric identifier. The cards would be checked against a national secure database, holding the information contained on the card and relevant biometric data, to confirm identity. According to the government, the scheme would provide individuals with a watertight 'proof of identity' and, as such, help to combat certain types of serious crime, such as terrorism and drug trafficking. . . .

Although the 2004 Bill did not survive the Parliamentary session 2004/05, it was re-introduced with only minor amendments in May 2005. It was passed in its third Commons reading on 18 October 2005 by 309 votes to 284 and proceeded to the House of Lords. The Lords proposed no fewer than 72 amendments to the Bill including an amendment which would have meant that individuals would not automatically be deemed to have applied to have their details entered in the Register and to be issued with an ID card when they applied for a 'designated document'. Most of the amendments were rejected when the Bill returned to the House of Commons in February 2006.

The Bill was always controversial. Civil liberties campaigners claim that the introduction of an identity card scheme "will have far reaching implications for the relationship between the individual and the state" and that ID cards will "intrude on privacy as the amount of information held on the database and the uses made of that information will increase dramatically". In October 2005, the Information Commissioner expressed concern about the extent to which the Bill would breach data protection principles. While the Government estimates the cost of implementing the system to be in the region of £5.6 billion, an independent study carried out by a team at the London School of Economics put the true cost between £12 billion and £18 billion. . . .

In view of the immense cost of the system and the doubts over its usefulness it is difficult to see how its introduction can justify the intrusion upon individual freedoms and privacy. Identity cards will certainly not prevent the commission of crimes by any person never previously involved in any criminal or terrorist activity. They will also not stop those with special skills and knowledge from manipulating database content in a way which would allow the production of fake identification and authentification instruments. As Dumbledore observed, any skilled terrorist is bound to make sure that he has obtained sufficient information before trying to impersonate another person. Rather than protecting the public from terrorism, a national database and identity card may, on the contrary, provide a means to those planning an attack for obtaining a bogus identity, thereby allowing them to circumvent brittle security systems which have a propensity to fail. It is at least possible that this could reduce rather than increase real security in the UK.

Security Theatre

> 'They probably want to look as if they're doing something', said Hermione, frowning. 'People are terrified'. [*Harry Potter and the Half-Blood Prince*]

As shown above, the Ministry of Magic, like the UK Government, has a desire to be seen to be doing something. Following a well publicised battle between Lord Voldemort's supporters and the members of a secret society dedicated to fighting him, the Ministry takes a number of allegedly protective steps. A new Minister for Magic is appointed and "tough new measures" are reportedly being taken "to ensure the safety of students returning to Hogwarts School". The leaflet titled "Protecting your home and your family against dark forces" issued to all wizarding households is another example of the way in which the Ministry attempts to reassure the frightened population.

As already mentioned, the security leaflet bears an uncanny resemblance to the leaflet "Preparing for Emergencies—what you need to know", produced by the UK Government and delivered to all UK households in 2005. Like the wizarding leaflet, the Government's advice was largely ignored when it arrived on people's doorstep. Undoubtedly, it was intended to be a PR exercise aiming to ease people's fears rather than providing real information which would be helpful in a crisis situation. Security expert Bruce Schneier calls such measures, which provide the feeling of security instead of the reality, 'security theatre' and 'palliative at best.' . . .

Civil Measures

> 'I warned Sirius when we adopted twelve Grimmauld Place as our Headquarters that Kreacher must be treated with kindness and respect. I also told him that Kreacher could be

> dangerous to us. I do not think that Sirius took me very seriously, or that he ever saw Kreacher as a being with feelings as acute as a human's. . . . Kreacher is what he has been made by wizards, Harry', said Dumbledore. 'Yes, he is to be pitied'. [*Harry Potter and the Order of the Phoenix*]

Throughout the series Rowling attempts to show how the attitude of the wizarding community towards minority groups has contributed to the problems it faces in relation to the Dark Arts. There is a strong feeling amongst many wizards not only of their superiority towards muggles and other wizards but also towards other human and non-human creatures. This causes friction in the wizarding society. For example, prejudice against giants and werewolves leads to these groups aligning themselves with Lord Voldemort. Centaurs are abused as 'filthy half-breeds' when in reality they represent a highly developed culture with an ability to divine future events. Finally, house elves enjoy the status of unpaid labourers in wizard households, much in the way of slaves or low paid servants in human society. Even Harry's godfather, Sirius Black, treats his house elf Kreacher with little more than disdain. This moves Kreacher to assist the Death Eaters in a plot which leads to Sirius' death. Although Harry and his friend Ron try to encounter all creatures with an open mind, it is only his friend Hermione—who, in *Harry Potter and the Goblet of Fire*, founds the Society for the Protection of Elfish Welfare—and Dumbledore, who really advocate greater interaction and understanding between the different cultures. Immediately after Voldemort's return to power, Dumbledore advises the Minister of Magic to make peace with the giants in an attempt to persuade them to join the wizarding community in their fight against the Dark Arts. The Minister refuses, arguing that he would be hounded out of office for suggesting it. Predictably, most of the giants later join Voldemort.

The reaction of Western states to the terrorist attacks of 11 September were equally mixed. While some employed a rhetoric of confrontation—speaking of a 'war on terror' fought by a 'coalition of the willing', others responded in a way which could be "characterised principally as a civil reaction" [states S. von Schorlemer]. Von Schorlemer explains:

> Most European states opted for what may be called a 'prevention' strategy, and underlined the importance of non-military measures to combat international terrorism, including an increase in development aid and economic cooperation and greater cooperation in international fora to ensure wider implementation of international human rights instruments. Thus there is a strong belief, in Europe at least, that terrorism cannot be defeated purely by military means and that it is necessary also to confront the underlying causes.

This approach was criticised by many in the US as appeasement politics and the states refusing to join the military coalition were ridiculed as 'old Europe'. However, more than four years after 9/11, it has become clear, that "the message given by western states of threat from other realms, especially the Islamic world", has encouraged "a response of equal intolerance" [according to C. Walker]. In a speech given at Harvard Law School on 8 March 2004, [the] then Home Secretary, David Blunkett, characterised the threat faced by contemporary society as one from 'franchised terror'. One could argue that the real threat is more likely to come from 'disenfranchised terror'. As [Paul] Hoffman, Chair of the International Executive Committee of Amnesty International, points out,

> a state's failure to adhere to fundamental human rights norms makes it more likely that terrorist organisations will find it easier to recruit adherents among the discontented and disenfranchised and among the family and friends of those whose human rights have been violated.

Human rights, along with democracy and social justice, "are seen as a means to prevent terrorism. Thus on this view, the key to enhancing security is the pursuit by all governments of a comprehensive human rights programme" [says S. von Schorlemer]. . . .

Parallels Between British Government and Wizards' Fights Against Terror

This paper has shown that there are significant parallels between the response of the British Government to the terrorist threat and the way in which J K Rowling portrays the wizarding community's fight against Lord Voldemort. It would be farfetched to call any of her books a roman à clef—she does not draw parallels to particular political players or historical proceedings. Rather, in a form of ironic plot-borrowing from current events, she draws our attention, very subtly, to areas where our society is in danger of becoming legally and morally deficient. Where she succeeds is in "capturing the spirit rather than the letter of life in these troubled times" [according to J. Taylor] and it is submitted that it is, among other things, this understated approach that makes her books so popular with the older generation.

Human Rights Are at the Core of Harry Potter

Rachel Dempsey

Rachel Dempsey, a staff writer for Amnesty International USA, finds the theme of ethnic cleansing to be central to Harry Potter and the Deathly Hallows. *The value of the book, she contends, is that it makes the issues of genocide and ethnic cleansing more accessible for children. Reading about genocide in the context of the Death Eaters helps children understand real-life atrocities such as the crisis in Sudan's Darfur region.*

A lot of the ideas in [*Harry Potter and the Deathly Hallows*]—about freedom of education, freedom of the press, and minority and indigenous rights—are similar to those in Book 5. Once again, the Ministry of Magic is controlling the curriculum at Hogwarts, Wizarding newspaper *The Daily Prophet* is functioning as a propaganda machine, and magical minorities are overlooked and disrespected by even decent people.

Some long-running plotlines come to a satisfying close. While Rowling has been poking gentle fun at activists for a while, in the form of the S.P.E.W. (Society to Promote Elvish Welfare) campaign, in Book 7 Hermione's clumsy efforts to raise the status of house-elves are vindicated. When Harry starts to treat house-elf Kreacher with respect, the formerly angry and vindictive creature warms to his new master. And Lord Voldemort's refusal to acknowledge the magical powers of elves proves his downfall when he fails to protect himself against the magic of non-wizards.

Rachel Dempsey, "Human Rights Summer Reading Series: *Harry Potter and the Deathly Hallows*," *Amnesty USA Blogs*, August 3, 2007. Author was an Amnesty International (AI) Intern. This article does not reflect the views of AI.

Ethnic Cleansing in *Deathly Hallows*

But the real human-rights core of *Harry Potter and the Deathly Hallows* emerges in its treatment of ethnic cleansing. The difference between pure-blood Wizards and Muggle-borns has been a constant theme throughout the entire Harry Potter series, but until Book 7 it was one undercurrent of many. . . .

In the final installment of the Harry Potter series, though, Voldemort takes control of the Ministry of Magic and embarks on a campaign to eliminate and punish "disloyal" Wizards. All Muggle-born Wizards are rounded up for questioning, and their names are put on a national register so they can be easily tracked.

I was particularly moved by the scene where Harry and Hermione stumble into the interrogation of a Muggle-born during a break-in at the Ministry of Magic. The allusions to real-life ethnic cleansing campaigns, from Cambodia to the Holocaust, couldn't be clearer.

Any epic of good-versus-evil is bound to elicit historical comparisons, and any historical insights drawn from a children's book are bound to be on the shallow side. Voldemort-as-Hitler is something of a cliche. Both of them have come to represent evil, as an abstract easy-to-hate concept, and drawing parallels is almost too easy.

But the novel part of what Rowling has managed to do, and what she truly deserves credit for, is making the problems of genocide and ethnic cleansing accessible for children too young to understand or care about the racial, religious and cultural persecution that, unfortunately, exists outside the world of fiction as well.

Attempting to explain [the conflict in the] Darfur [region of Sudan] to a child is no easy task. Using the Death Eaters as a parallel to the Janjawid [Arab militias that have been accused of committing genocide in Darfur] is a gross oversimplification of an extremely complicated situation, but ironically, placing genocide in the fictional world of Harry Potter can help make it more real. So if you have a kid, or know a kid, who is reading *Harry Potter and the Deathly Hallows*, try to engage them in a discussion of the human rights themes in the book.

Chapter 3

Contemporary Perspectives on Political Issues

Children's Fears of Terrorism Increased After 9/11

Joy J. Burnham

Joy J. Burnham, assistant professor of counselor education at the University of Alabama, examined the fears of children both prior to and following the September 11, 2001, terrorist attacks on the United States. Her objectives were to compare general fears and terror-related fears during the two periods. Her study showed that while general fears remained stable during the two periods, fears related to terrorism significantly increased following 9/11. She also found that younger children were the most fearful, and girls were more frightened of terrorist attacks than boys.

On September 11, 2001, hijacked commercial airplanes flew into the World Trade Center towers and the Pentagon and attempted to attack a third target. The events were described as "the most deadly terrorist acts ever to occur in the United States" [by psychologist W. Schlenger and others]. After these terrorist attacks, many researchers examined how this unprecedented act of terror affected children. Approximately 6 months after 9/11, 1 in 4 of 8,000 New York City children studied had anxiety and emotional symptoms related to the attacks, suggesting that they would benefit from mental health services. In another study, [M.A.] Schuster [and others] surveyed a randomly selected group of 768 parents to see what they perceived were their children's responses to 9/11. The results demonstrated "substantial symptoms of stress" among their children including "(1) avoiding talking or hearing about what happened, (2) having trouble keeping his or

Joy J. Burnham, "Children's Fears: A Pre-9/11 and Post-9/11 Comparison Using the American Fear Survey Schedule for Children," *Journal of Counseling & Development*, vol. 85, Fall 2007, pp. 461–465.

her mind on things and concentrating, (3) having trouble falling asleep or staying asleep, (4) losing his or her temper or being irritable, and (5) having nightmares."

Children have typical responses in postdisaster situations. [J.M.] Vogel and [E.M.] Vernberg noted that a "fear of reoccurrence is one of the most general postdisaster responses" for children. These authors also illustrated that fears can be broad and complex, such as "intrusive reexperiencing, attempts to avoid reminders, and arousal of PTSD [post-traumatic stress disorder] syndrome as a type of extreme prolonged fear response." Vogel and Vernberg also described an inverse relationship involving children's fears. They concluded that children's fears directly related to the disaster will increase in frequency and intensity, whereas fears unrelated to the disaster or trauma will not increase in the postdisaster time frame. Based on this theory, it could be postulated that after 9/11, fears related to terrorist attacks would increase, but overall general fears (e.g., snakes, school-related fears, spooky things) would not increase. . . .

Methodology of Survey

The current study had two objectives. The first objective was to compare overall fears and terror-related intensity fear scores (i.e., pre-9/11 to post-9/11) on the American Fear Survey Schedule for Children [FSSC-AM]. The second objective was to investigate whether or not the data substantiate the following postulations found in the literature: (a) Fears specifically related to a disaster will increase after the event and (b) general fears unrelated to the disaster will not increase after the traumatic event.

The pre-9/11 data were collected in 1995 in 18 schools (Grades 2–12) in two southeastern states. . . .

The post-9/11 data were collected in 16 schools (Grades 2–12) in two southeastern states between November 2001 and February 2003. . . .

Participants responded to each of the 98 fear items with one of the following choices: *not scared* (1), *scared* (2), or *very scared* (3). A total overall fear intensity score was obtained by summing the scores across all fear items. A total terror score was obtained by summing the scores of the 9 terror fear items on the FSSC-AM. The terror fear items were "our country being invaded by enemies," "nuclear war," "murderers," "flying in a plane," "being threatened with a gun," "terrorist attacks," "having to fight in a war," "drive-by shootings," and "people carrying guns/knives/weapons."...

Results of Survey

As the first pretest and posttest examination of the 9/11 terrorist attacks using [what E. Gullone called] "exclusive assessment tool for fear assessment," this study revealed new findings and subsequently supported previous postdisaster studies. By using the terror fear items on the FSSC-AM, meaningful inferences were made about fears of youth who were distant from 9/11. In the past, most disaster-related fear studies have considered children who were near disasters. The results of this study indicate that more research is needed on youth who are exposed to disasters but located at a "safe distance" from the actual disaster site. Examining youth in other geographic regions of the United States is also indicated.

Several conclusions were notable. The pre-9/11 and post-9/11 fear intensity scores for all fear items on the FSSC-AM were not significantly different. This aspect of the study revealed similarities in overall general fears between the pre-9/11 and post-9/11 samples. The conclusion also supports previous work [that] posited that general fears do not increase after a disaster. Thus, it can be surmised that the general fears of this population of students were stable during the tumultuous months after September 11, 2001. Conversely, the 9 terror fears on the FSSC-AM showed significant increases post-9/11, which also corroborated with past research. By comparing pre-9/11 and post-9/11 years, the results indicated that post-9/11 participants were significantly more fearful of "our country being invaded by enemies," "terrorist attacks," and "flying in a plane" than were pre-9/11 participants. Thus, specific disaster-related fears increased after 9/11 in this study, similar to findings in past studies. The significant post-9/11 terror fear increases reinforced previous 9/11 studies that were completed near disaster sites. Further examination of the interaction of the fear items "our country being invaded by enemies," "terrorist attacks," and "flying in a plane" at the post-9/11 measurement revealed that boys and girls in three age groups were significantly more frightened of "our country being invaded by enemies" and "terrorist attacks" than were their counterparts at the pre-9/11 measurement. This was compelling, not only for the significance of the 2 fear items, but also because boys rarely report higher fears than girls. Studies have shown for decades that girls overwhelmingly report more fears than boys on self-report fear instruments. By investigating the gender, age group, and year effects, more light was shed on the influences of 9/11. The gender effect supported typical trends in fear research literature that indicate higher endorsements of fears for girls than for boys. In the current study, girls were significantly more fearful of "our country being invaded by enemies," "terrorist attacks," and "flying in a plane" than were boys. The current study also affirmed typical developmental fear patterns indicating that fears decrease as children mature with age. For example, the fears of "our country being invaded by enemies" and "terrorist attacks" decreased for the sample of older children, suggesting that the children in primary grades were the most frightened, scared and confused after 9/11. By comparing the pre-9/11 and post-9/11 test years, the results indicated that pre-9/11 participants were significantly more fearful of "our country being invaded by enemies," "terrorist attacks," and "flying in a plane" than were pre-9/11 participants.

Overall, meaningful conclusions and practical applications can be drawn from the findings of the current study for mental health counselors, school counselors, psychologists, and other helping professionals who work with children and adolescents. Studies in the past have shown that traumatic events stimulate anxiety and fear in children. Furthermore, conclusions from past studies indicate that distant trauma effects, even PTSD symptoms, can be found in children who are distant from disasters. The current study found that the 9/11 events significantly aroused fear levels for post-9/11 youth residing in the southeastern United States, distant in proximity to Washington, DC and New York City. Similar to [L.C.] Terr et al.'s assumptions of distant trauma resulting from television exposure, it can be assumed that television exposure to 9/11 had a strong, negative impact on the youth in the current study, particularly the younger children. The connection between fears and developmental theory was also observed. The terrorist attacks were most vivid and scary for the young children because of their developmental stage.

Implications of Results

There were numerous implications to be drawn from the current study. Young children were the most frightened participants in this study, likely because of their cognitive development at the time of 9/11, indicating that screening procedures and interventions may be necessary for them after exposure to traumatic events. Nonetheless, counseling resources for all grade levels at school and in the community are beneficial after major disasters occur (e.g., school counseling interventions, mental health professionals at school, service providers in the community). As [E.R.] DeVoe et al. reiterated, the need for "developmentally relevant mental health services" to be made available to children and parents "in the aftermath of a significant community trauma like 9/11" was evident in this study. Furthermore, with the significance of television in the lives of youth (i.e., a means by which many participants gained knowledge of 9/11), counselors should advocate for the "less is better" perspective on media coverage after trauma. Therefore, counselors should encourage parents to limit television viewing of the coverage of traumatic events.

Studies of the effects of disasters and tragedies that have occurred during the past 20 years have taught that youth are influenced by the salient events surrounding them. The examples given in the current study offer a glimpse of the fears and anxieties that were manifested for children and adolescents after 9/11, even in communities far away from the disaster sites. In the future, being cognizant of these findings should avert certain negative impacts on children and adolescents.

Suspending Civil Liberties Does Not Stop Terrorism

Leonard Pitts Jr.

Leonard Pitts Jr. contends that the CIA's destruction of videotapes that allegedly depict the brutal interrogation of terrorist suspects is another example of the United States' inclination to curtail civil liberties when people are scared. He cites other turbulent times in history when civil liberties were violated, including the civil rights movement, the Red scare, and the Japanese invasion of Pearl Harbor. A better response, he suggests, is not to give in to our fears but to stand up for what we believe in. Pitts, a nationally syndicated columnist for the Miami Herald, *won the Pulitzer Prize for Commentary in 2004. He is the author of* Becoming Dad: Black Men and the Journey to Fatherhood *(1999).*

The authorities would just come into your home, grab your mother, your brother, your dad and take them away. No warning, no warrant, no appeal.

Thirty thousand people were disappeared that way, she told me. This was in an interview three years ago, and Ruth Cox was describing her childhood in Argentina under military dictatorship. Cox, a teacher in Charleston, S.C., said families never learned what happened to their loved ones. Or why. People were taken and that was it. The government was not accountable.

My first response was a vague pride that those kinds of things can't happen here.

My second response was to realize that my first response was naive. These last years have provided a jolting education

Leonard Pitts Jr., "Years after 9/11, Nation Remains Scared," The *Miami Herald*, January 6, 2008.

in the sorts of things that can, indeed, happen here. Mass surveillance, detention without access to courts, no right to confront, or even know, the evidence against you, torture. And a government that is not accountable.

News [in early 2008] that the Justice Department has launched a criminal investigation into the CIA's destruction of videotapes said to depict the harsh interrogation of terrorism suspects is welcome, but also belated, the very embodiment of the old saw about locking the garage after the car's been stolen. Though we have lost a lot more than a car.

Violation of Civil Liberties Is a Reaction to Fear

And here, a line from a Bruce Springsteen song seems apropos. "The flag flying over the courthouse means certain things are set in stone. Who we are, and what we'll do and what we won't." Sadly, the list of what we won't do has narrowed dramatically since 2001.

It's telling that a number of politicians have lately cited as their model on terrorism issues Jack Bauer, the counterterrorism agent on the TV hit *24*, who routinely tortures the truth out of bad guys as the clock ticks toward catastrophe. It's not hard to understand the appeal. There's a certain atavistic attraction to the Jack Bauer method, an attraction that bypasses the head en route to the gut.

Too bad, because had the head been asked, it might have pointed out that Jack Bauer is a fictional character on a TV show not noted for its realism. Using him as a guide to terrorism makes about as much sense as using Barney Fife [a character from the 1960s television program *The Andy Griffith Show*] as a guide to law enforcement.

And the very fact that Jack Bauer is invoked in the most crucial policy debate of our time tells you something about the state of the union going on seven years after the Sept. 11 attacks. In a word: scared.

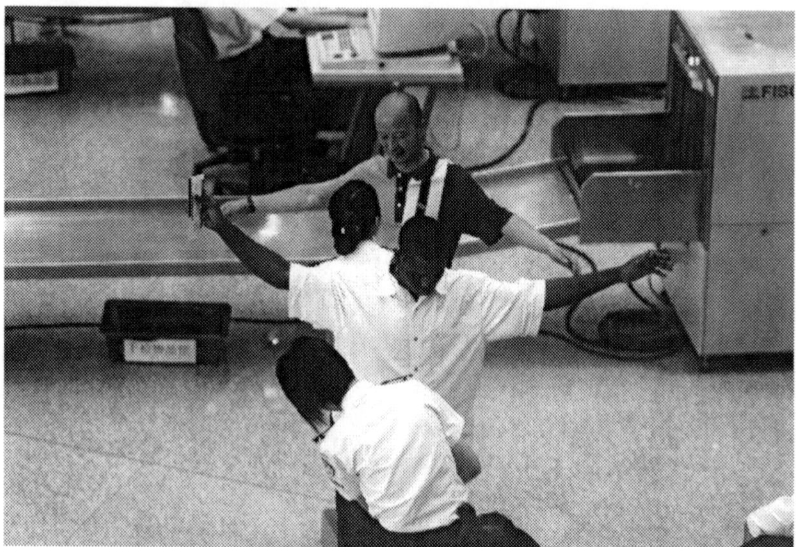

Years after the 9/11 attacks, airport security and fear remain high for further attempts by terrorists. AP Images.

There is nothing new about being scared. Nor about abridging civil liberties in response. It happened in the civil rights movement, in the Red scare, happened when the Japanese attacked Pearl Harbor, when the nation plunged into World War I, when John Adams was offended by the French.

But it's worth noting that, for all the illegal wiretapping, arrests, detention, blacklisting, censorship and loss of life this country has seen in the name of fear, only one major abridgement of civil liberties in time of national emergency—Lincoln's suspension of habeas corpus during the Civil War—stands justified by hindsight.

The rest, we regard with a shamefaced fascination. We wonder what we were thinking, how we wandered so far afield from the principles that should make us great.

We'll wonder this time, too.

And me, I also wonder this: Are we doomed to keep learning the same lesson every generation? Or will we finally decide someday to stand for what we stand for even—*especially*—

when we are scared? That kind of courage might not stop terrorists, but it could cripple *terrorism*.

Because violence that intends to instill fear is not the only threat we face. We are also threatened by the fear itself. Fear is the enemy of reason. Fear can leave you fundamentally changed.

It can't happen here, I said.

But of course, it already has.

Terrorism Needs to Be Fought with Military Goals and Advancement of Human Rights

Paul Starr, Michael Tomasky, and Robert Kuttner

In the following viewpoint, the authors contend that the Bush administration's failed foreign policy gives liberals the opportunity to propose an alternative. They believe that George W. Bush exited Afghanistan without accomplishing the intended mission—of killing Osama bin Laden—and then diverted forces to Iraq to launch a war based on false premises. As a result, terrorists remain a threat and the United States is engaged in a war unpopular at home and abroad. The proposed alternative is to develop a foreign policy that combines liberalism with realism. Instead of following the Bush administration's practice of acting unilaterally, the authors suggest that the United States needs to work cooperatively with other countries to help advance democracy and civil liberties throughout the world and, at the same time, respond with military force to any threat of terrorism. Paul Starr and Robert Kuttner are coeditors of the American Prospect. *Michael Tomasky is the editor of the online newspaper* Guardian America. *Starr is the author of* Freedom's Power: The True Force of Liberalism; *Kuttner's publications include* The Squandering of America: How the Failure of Our Politics Undermines Our Prosperity.

It is a shame there will never be a debate about foreign policy between the George W. Bush who ran for president in 2000 and the one who now occupies the office. As a candidate five years ago, Bush said that the United States should act

Paul Starr, Michael Tomasky, and Robert Kuttner, "The Liberal Uses of Power," *The American Prospect*, March 2005. Reproduced with permission from The American Prospect, 11 Beacon Street, Suite 1120, Boston, MA 02108.

as a "humble nation" toward the rest of the world and avoid any involvement of our armed forces in nation building. He could have had a lively argument with the current president [in 2005] over the use of the military for nation building in Iraq, and he might have raised an eyebrow over the president's declaration, at his second inauguration, that it is American policy to "seek and support the growth of democratic movements and institutions in every nation and culture, with the ultimate goal of ending tyranny in our world." The original Bush appealed to an insular Americanism with a constricted conception of the national interest; the new Bush appeals to a missionary vision of America's role. As much as the first understated America's obligations, the second risks overextending them. In our hypothetical debate, the two would nonetheless find they had a lot in common: an us-and-them view of good and evil in the world; an indifference toward allies and international institutions; and, of course, a readiness to use force.

Terrorists Are Still a Threat

Bush's worldview and instincts served the country well enough in the immediate aftermath of September 11 [2001], at least with respect to foreign policy: The terrorists were indeed evil, and the war in Afghanistan was a fully justified response. But the limitations of the president's approach to the world have been evident ever since. He undertook the Iraq War on false and misleading premises, with overoptimistic expectations and inadequate post-invasion plans, undermining our credibility, alliances, and focus on al-Qaeda. It was only as his original rationale for invading Iraq weakened and ultimately collapsed that he reframed the war as a crusade for democracy. If the Iraqis now establish a stable, democratic government, it will be a great positive step for their country and the region, but there is a considerable risk of an unintended and perverse result: a pro-Iranian Islamic state hostile to liberal values and

American interests and willing to hold free elections only as long as they produce results acceptable to the Shia clerical hierarchy.

Moreover, even if Iraq's government does not go the way of Iran, the Iraq War will not have removed the perils that led to the direct engagement of the United States in the Islamic world. Three and a half years after September 11, Islamist terrorists remain a threat, U.S. military forces are stretched to the limit, anti-Americanism has intensified in Europe and the Middle East, and our traditional allies are increasingly distrustful of U.S. leadership and are setting an independent path in foreign affairs.

In other ways, the Bush administration has also undermined American power and influence. Its fiscal policies have created a dangerous dependence on foreign borrowing to finance our budget and trade deficits, and its energy policies have increased our dependence on foreign oil. The inevitable result is a double standard vis-à-vis China and unsavory Middle Eastern regimes. Bush's defenders like to portray liberals, particularly those who opposed the Iraq War, as weak and unserious about national security. But the truth is that the war itself and other administration policies are weakening our power and security, undermining our alliances and freedom of action.

America Should Be a Force for Good

These problems with the administration's policies—and the absence of an overall strategy in foreign affairs from today's Democratic leaders—invite liberals to offer a compelling alternative in the spirit of Franklin Delano Roosevelt, Harry Truman, George Kennan, Dean Acheson, and John F. Kennedy. Mixing liberalism with realism in foreign policy, these leaders were not afraid to use power. They knew when to apply military force, when to "arm to parley" (as Kennedy liked to quote [Winston] Churchill), when to use diplomacy backed by the threat of force, and when to pursue genuinely humanitarian initiatives such as the Peace Corps—the 1960s' version of "soft power"—to further American interests. In that tradition, we believe that America can and should be an assertive force for good in the world. And, as liberals, we also believe that America faces a mortal threat from Islamist terrorists that will require every asset we can bring to bear, including military force.

In his second inaugural address, the president [Bush] set out an attractive vision of the United States as a liberator of oppressed nations. Woodrow Wilson and FDR would have recognized the sentiments. We can imagine a Democrat in Bush's place upholding the same aspirations (though the Republican reception would have been altogether different); indeed, we anticipate that liberals in the future will have more occasion to quote Bush's speech than conservatives will. But the president's glittering generalities were not a policy. Will freedom now weigh more heavily than trade in our relations with China? More heavily than stability in our relations with Pakistan or Egypt? More heavily than support for the war on terrorism in our relations with Russia? If the speech signaled no change in policy—as senior White House advisers said afterward—was it merely another retrospective justification of the Iraq War? Was it the first shot in a new war aimed at regime change, this time in Iran? Or did it serve mainly to obscure the real nature of the policy toward the world that Bush is pursuing?

While trumpeting the spread of democracy, Bush has also claimed a singular position for the United States. The administration has repudiated long-standing principles of international law, downgraded multilateral institutions, and rejected a series of international treaties regarding the International Criminal Court, global warming, and other issues. The United States emerged from the 1990s as an overwhelmingly dominant military power, and to the rest of the world, Bush now

U.S. soldiers help evacuees flee rising floodwaters in South Cotabato in the southern Philippines on June 21, 2008. Mark Navales/AFP/Getty Images.

appears intent on exploiting that position to advance American interests and demand exemptions from the rules that other nations follow. Growing opposition to U.S. policy was already on the rise throughout Europe and elsewhere in the world long before Iraq. In much of the world, the banner of democracy looks like a deceptive cover for American hegemony.

A Liberal Alternative to Bush's Policies

In reaction against Bush's embrace of Wilsonian rhetoric, some liberals may be tempted to go to the opposite extreme, downplaying any democratic aims of American foreign policy and asserting only the goals of peace and stability. That is not our view. In charting an alternative to Bush's foreign policy, liberals should uphold liberal aims. But those aims are not well served by a policy that has discarded the framework of international law and institutions built up since World War II and has made American power appear illegitimate in the eyes even of traditional allies. We need to distinguish carefully between what realism demands in the short run, particularly when dealing with terrorism, and longer-term possibilities for freedom in the world. Those possibilities ought to include the advance of democracy and human rights, along with goals entirely missing from the Bush administration's agenda, such as the protection of the global environment and the reduction of global poverty.

The first imperative of America's defense and foreign policy, however, is to protect our security, and today Islamist terrorists with global reach pose the greatest immediate threat to our lives and liberties. We—the United States, the advanced world generally, and liberals in particular, who value the rule of law, equality, open-mindedness, tolerance, and secularism—face a struggle with the jihadists that we have no alternative but to win. The fanatical nature of Islamic fundamentalism and the terrorism it has spawned should be clear to all of us. Its goals for the world are so profoundly inimical to ours, and its methods so intolerable, that negotiation, of the sort the United States engaged in with its best-known ideological foe of the last century, is impossible. The terrorists not only threaten liberal values in Islamic countries; they also imperil the survival of freedom in ours. If they launch further major attacks on our shores, the PATRIOT Act and Guantanamo Bay will likely prove mere prelude to much worse. Defending our liberties and best traditions at home, then, depends directly on defeating terrorism abroad.

Our call for clarity in dealing with terrorism reflects the urgency of a historical moment that demands we sort out the things that are genuinely important—the conditions that are necessary for the flourishing of liberal values. The lines that separate liberal principle from fundamentalist design have rarely been clearer, and they are lines that liberals must defend unambiguously, and with force when necessary. President Bush has been wrong, often calamitously so, about many things, but he is right that America must do all it can to prevent another 9-11. When facing a substantial, immediate, and provable threat, the United States has both the right and the obligation to strike preemptively and, if need be, unilaterally against terrorists or states that support them.

Disagreement Among Liberals

Because of the direct threat of Islamic terrorism to liberal values, liberals ought to be particularly conscious of the need for an effective defense. But some have drawn the wrong lessons from history. Beginning with the Vietnam War, many progressives instinctively opposed any assertion of American power. They pointed, accurately enough, to instances where the United States engineered the overthrow of democratically elected left-wing governments while supporting dictators of convenience, such as the shah of Iran. After Saddam Hussein invaded Kuwait in 1990, too few liberals saw that a war was a just and necessary response. Many, however, were more favorable to the use of force later in the decade, when Bill Clinton's interventions in Bosnia and Kosovo stopped ethnic cleansing and prevented Serbian aggression from spiraling into a wider war in the region. September 11 solidified the growing conviction among liberals that the United States had to be prepared to use force to defend security and liberal values.

Still, some on the left opposed the war in Afghanistan, and just as Vietnam led to an overly broad rejection of force, so the misconceived invasion of Iraq now lends credence to a reflexive hostility to American power. We understand the historical roots of this mistrust, but today's world presents problems that require different habits of mind. The real problem in Afghanistan was not that the United States sent in troops but that it did not send in enough to complete the job and capture or kill Osama bin Laden. Iraq was the wrong war waged the wrong way; it began on false premises and may end badly—but we can neither walk away from it nor become complacent about other dangers.

Liberals are bound to disagree about these questions, and sometimes disagree strenuously. Lobbing rhetorical grenades at one another is always a tempting pleasure; recently, liberal hawks seem especially to be enjoying the sport, to the harrumphing approval of commentators on the right. But, at the end of the day, liberals have to offer an alternative capable of dislodging neoconservatism as the nation's governing ideology. That alternative can embrace, in our view, both a commitment to building an international structure of cooperation and a recognition that, where terrorism is concerned, preemptive, unilateral, and decisive force may be legitimate.

The right of preemption, however, is not the same as a blanket entitlement to preventive war to overthrow hostile regimes that pose no immediate threat, particularly where other countermeasures, international in scope, may be sufficient to achieve the purpose. As the Iraq experience shows, mistakes in preventive war have enormous costs in the lost credibility of American leadership, lost resources, and, not least of all, lost lives. The United States has unmatched military power, but our armed forces are relatively limited in numbers, and even this country will find itself overextended if it tries to use force to squelch all potential threats.

Addressing Root Causes of Terrorism

The larger problem, moreover, arises from the environment that has fostered terrorism. The jihadists can lay claim, it is sad to observe, to deep intellectual roots in the Muslim world, the indirect support of schools and cultural institutions, and a significant body of public opinion. A resolution of the Israeli-Palestinian conflict would help remove a major source of inflammation between Islamic fundamentalism and the West, but the terrorist threat wouldn't end there. We have a stake in the success of liberalizing educational and cultural forces in the Islamic world, and we ought to be using our resources and influence to bolster those movements.

Some liberal hawks today invoke the liberal anti-communists of the Cold War as a model for the struggle against the jihadists, but the analogy would support their position, including the invasion of Iraq, only if the United States had triumphed over the Soviet Union by attacking and "rolling back" communism. In fact, success in the Cold War came as a result of containment, deterrence, multilateralism, and patience—liberal policies tempered by realism. The Cold War, however, offers us only an inexact parallel for the challenge we face today. Containment and negotiation will not suffice against terrorist networks; we are effectively in a state of war against them and must use every means available to bring about their defeat. But even in that struggle, we need the strongest possible international cooperation and legitimacy, and the legacy of international institutions from the Cold War provides us with a foundation and a model for further efforts.

As the sole superpower in the world, the United States is in an extraordinary position to shape the rules and practices of the international system. That system can augment our power, as it did during the Cold War, through a system of partnerships with other countries, based on consultation and joint decision making. Instead, under Bush's leadership, the United States is intent on setting a unilateral course, which other countries are welcome to join if they accept our terms. That approach appeals to a deep, conservative nationalist tendency in America. From the insular conservatism that Bush advocated in 2000, it is but a short step to the missionary neoconservatism that he espouses today. Both are dismissive of a cooperative international framework. But acting unilaterally, the United States will face twin problems of its own making at home and abroad. First, as in Iraq, American taxpayers will assume an outsized share of the military burden of maintaining world order. And second, we will continue generating hostility elsewhere in the world and spurring other countries, including our traditional allies, to do what they have already begun: strengthen their own partnerships, like the European Union, separate from and perhaps increasingly in opposition to us. The liberal alternative to Bush is not to lessen our power but to listen to the world and, in the process, to add to the power that we and other liberal democracies can marshal to strengthen our security and freedom and to get on with the forgotten agenda of protecting the global environment and alleviating the poverty and misery that are still the fate of hundreds of millions of the world's people.

Ethnic Separation Is a Nonviolent Form of Ethnic Cleansing

Ralph Peters

Ralph Peters, a retired Army officer, points out there is a difference between genocide, which attempts to exterminate a minority, and ethnic cleansing, which attempts to expel a minority. He argues that while ethnic cleansing is never desirable, a milder version of it in the form of ethnic separation may be the best alternative in situations where ethnic groups are unable to live in harmony. The author contends that by trying to hold the rest of the world to our idealized standards of ethnic harmony, the United States has contributed to the destabilization of parts of the world from the Balkans to Iraq. Peters urges a more pragmatic approach to prevent all-out genocide. He is a columnist and strategist and the author of Wars of Blood and Faith: The Conflicts That Will Shape the 21st Century.

Ethnic cleansing is evil. It can never be condoned. Yet our repugnance at the act leaves us with a dilemma: What are we supposed to do in cases where ethnic cleansing may be impossible to prevent—cases in which well-intentioned efforts to interrupt ethnic cleansing actually make a conflict deadlier?

Ethnic Cleansing Differs from Genocide

One problem we face is a muddle in terminology, employing "ethnic cleansing" and "genocide" interchangeably; in fact, there is a profound difference between these two human habits. Genocide is the attempt to *exterminate* a minority. Ethnic cleansing seeks to *expel* a minority. At its less serious end, eth-

Ralph Peters, "Better Than Genocide," *National Review*, vol. 59, August 13, 2007, pp. 35–37.

nic cleansing may aim only at the separation of populations deemed incompatible by at least one side, with psychological, legalistic, or financial machinations brought to bear to achieve the desired end. At the other extreme, ethnic cleansing can involve deadly violence and widespread abuse. In the worst cases, ethnic-cleansing efforts may harden into genocide.

It must never become the policy of the United States to abet ethnic cleansing. Yet our all-or-nothing reaction when confronted with this common human phenomenon has proven to be consistently ineffective, from the Balkans to Iraq. Until we make an honest attempt to understand the age-old human impulse to rid a troubled society of those who are different in ethnicity or religion, we will continue to fail in our efforts to pacify and repair war-ravaged territories. If our conflicts over the past decade and a half offer any lesson, it's that the rest of the world refuses to conform to our idealized notions of how human beings are designed to behave. We never stop insisting that the peoples of the former Yugoslavia, the tribes of Somalia, the ethnic groups of Afghanistan, and, most painfully, the religious and ethnic factions of Iraq learn to live in harmony. Those we hope to convince ignore us.

If ethnic cleansing can be prevented and the society rejuvenated, that's an admirable accomplishment. But not all enraged passions can be calmed, no matter how vociferously we insist otherwise. Once ignited, some human infernos must burn themselves out; and you had best position any firebreaks correctly. To date, our reactions to situations in which ethnic cleansing cannot be arrested have been inept; in Iraq, for example, well-intentioned attempts to stymie neighborhood ethnic-cleansing efforts may have led to the targets' being murdered as opposed to merely forcibly removed. We struggle to keep families in their homes; in response, the families are massacred in those homes. We pretend that embedded hatreds are transient misunderstandings, but we're not the victims who pay the price for our fantasies.

As uncomfortable as it may be to face the facts, ethnic cleansing has been a deeply ingrained response of human collectives since the dawn of history, and it's preferable to uncompromising genocide.

Ethnic Cleansing Has a Long History

Why do human collectives feel compelled to expel neighbors with whom they may have lived in relative peace for generations, or even centuries? It's a difficult question. The Western model of studying the individual and then extrapolating our findings to the society prevents us from understanding mass behavior, which is far more complex (and murky) than the sum of individual actions. In much of the world—not least, in the Middle East—a more incisive approach is to examine the mass first, then extrapolate to the individual. We're astonished when foreign actors we know as affable individuals are swept up in mob behavior, but the mob may be their natural element and the reasonable character we encountered on a personal level a fragile aberration: Even in our own society, the mass remains more powerful than the man.

A related obstacle to understanding the insidious appeal of ethnic cleansing is that our leaders and opinion-makers interact disproportionately with foreign urban residents who have a higher education level, a greater English-language ability, and a more cosmopolitan outlook than the rest of their society. As a result, we're instructed that a given society doesn't support ethnic cleansing, since there are mixed marriages in Sarajevo or Baghdad or Weimar Germany. But the impulse to expel those who are visibly or behaviorally different—or who are merely accused of being different—is deeply rooted in the human soil. The man in the mansion may tell you one thing, but the unemployed citizen out on the street may bring to bear a very different psychology—along with an inchoate desire for vengeance inseparable from the human condition.

In the Old Testament, you can search fruitlessly through book after book for an example of disparate populations living happily side by side as equals. Ethnic cleansing and genocide appear early and continuously; and it is the differences between the various nationalities and tribes, not the commonalities, that are stressed in the foundational text of our civilization. We read not of a multicultural, tolerant society, but of a chosen people charged to conquer. Tribal genocides erupted throughout history when competition for scarce resources intensified; genocide is fundamentally Darwinian, as one group seeks to annihilate another for its own safety or other perceived benefits. Above the tribal level, though, full-scale genocides have been relatively rare; the more common practice, even in the case of the ever-cited Mongols, was selective mass-murder to instill fear—the slaughter of a city's population to persuade other cities not to resist.

The Romans knew how to punish convincingly, but had little taste for outright genocide. Their preference was for forms of ethnic cleansing that resettled troublesome tribes or dispersed rebellious populations—such as the Jews, following the rebellions of the first century A.D. (The Greeks, whose "civilized" behavior was a myth, had been more apt to slaughter rivals, whether in the poetry of Homer or the reportage of Thucydides.) From the Babylonian captivity, down to Stalin's practice of uprooting restive groups (such as the Chechens), ethnic cleansing as a tool of statecraft has a long, if hardly proud, tradition, with genocide reserved as the fail-safe answer.

Further confounding our preconceptions, state-organized programs of ethnic cleansing, for all their heartlessness, look relatively humane compared with the countless outbreaks of ethnic or religious cleansing inspired by roving demagogues, *agents provocateurs*, or simply rumors. While state genocide is the most potent form, state-backed ethnic cleansing tends to be less lethal than popular pogroms, since the state seeks to solve a perceived problem, while the mob wants blood (the horrific genocide perpetrated against the Armenians fatally combined state policy and popular bigotry in a muddle of genocide and ethnic cleansing). Once the people of a troubled society get it into their heads that their neighbors who look or sound or worship differently are enemies bent on subversion, outbursts of extraordinary savagery are the norm.

Ethnic Cleansing May Be the "Least Horrific" Alternative

In this context, ethnic cleansing might be the least horrific of the alternatives. Which atrocity was worse, the French massacre of Protestant Huguenots in the 16th century, or Louis XIV's expulsion of them in the 17th (a process that harmed the French economy, while benefiting German-speaking states)? The Spanish expulsions of the Jews and then the Moors were a vast human tragedy that ravaged Iberian civilization—but weren't those forced exiles preferable to Hitler's attempt to exterminate European Jewry? Even at the extremes of man-wrought evil, there are gradations of cruelty.

The historical evidence is troubling, since it suggests that ethnic cleansing can lead to peace. For example, the German presence amid Slavic populations in northeastern Europe lasted for eight oppressive centuries before all ethnic Germans were expelled in the wake of the Nazi collapse; after almost a millennium of torment, the region now enjoys an unprecedented level of peace and social justice. Certainly, other factors influenced this new calm—but the subtraction of Baltic, Ukrainian, Pomeranian, Silesian, and Sudeten Germans from the social and political equations appears to have been decisive.

In the wake of World War I, Greece and the Turkish rump of the Ottoman Empire exchanged millions of ethnic Turks and Greeks, under miserable conditions. The ethnic cleansing was harsh on both sides and the suffering of these hereditary enemies was immense. Yet, despite their history of violent antagonism, Greeks and Turks have remained at peace for more than eight decades since those mass expulsions, with the conflict over Cyprus confined to that unhappy island.

Meanwhile, trouble spots in which populations remain intermingled continue to erupt in violence, from West Africa through the Middle East to the Subcontinent and Southeast Asia (where anti-Chinese pogroms are almost as predictable as the monsoon season).

Nor can we Americans claim perfect innocence when it comes to ethnic cleansing. Our treatment of Native Americans remains, along with slavery and its consequences, one of the two great stains upon our history. And our present situation goes unexamined: On one hand, the unprecedented degree of ethnic and religious integration we have achieved (largely in the last half-century) blinds us to the depth and operative power of hatreds elsewhere in the world; on the other, our own society has devised innovative, relatively benign forms of achieving ethnic separation. The "gentrification" of neighborhoods in cities such as Washington, D.C., is a soft form of ethnic cleansing by checkbook and mortgage.

There is also an enduring self-segregation of various groups within our society. Many individuals prefer the familiarity and sense of security delivered by a collective identity, by the codes and symbols of belonging, whether displayed in a barrio or in the economic segregation of a suburban gated community. Even in our remarkable multi-ethnic, multiconfessional society, there are still race riots—in the course of which interlopers whose skin is the wrong color end up beaten beyond recognition or dead.

Human collectives are still, essentially, warrior bands protective of their turf (even in those gated communities—just attend a homeowners' association meeting). Group competition is powerfully embedded in our psyches. Successful societies channel such impulses constructively, but struggling societies and those that have already succumbed to anarchy revert to narrow (and safe) identities—race, tribe, faith, cult—and respond to perceived threats with assertive group behavior: The individual is lost once the group is awakened. We can deny it as often as we like, but the historical pattern is timeless and enduring: When the majority feels threatened, it lashes out at minorities in its midst. When a minority's ethnicity and religion *both* differ from the mainstream of a traditional society, that minority is living on borrowed time. The span of imagined safety may last for centuries, but then, one day, the zealots appear on the street corner, whether in brown shirts or wearing Islamist robes.

The Practical Implications of Ethnic Cleansing

It cannot be stressed too often or too forcefully that ethnic cleansing is a crime against humanity that cannot be excused. The purpose of this essay is to try to understand it—not to condone it—and to consider the implications for our military and diplomatic missions abroad.

Given that we would prefer to prevent any ethnic cleansing, what do we do when it cannot be prevented, when the hatred is too intense and the process already has gone too far? While there will never be a universal answer, given the complexity of each specific case, it can be argued as a case study that ethnic separation at an earlier stage might have prevented the massacre at Srebrenica (of course, no such separations will ever be fully just). Indeed, U.S. diplomats gave tacit approval to the Croatian cleansing of Serbs during the endgame in Croatia and Bosnia. Later, in Kosovo, we sought to persuade Serbs not to drive ethnic Albanians from their homes, but, as soon as victory was delivered to the Kosovars, they set about ethnically cleansing Serbs with high-testosterone vigor. The dynamic in play was such that none of our pleas, lectures, or scoldings were going to alter the hardened attitudes prevailing in either camp. What if the *only* hope for peace in the territory some still pretend is a unified Kosovo is ethnic separation and partition?

Meanwhile, in Iraq, ethnic-cleansing efforts have been savage. They still fall short of genocide: Confessional murders to date have aimed at intimidation and expulsion, at punishment and advantage, not at annihilation. What if the best hope for social peace is the establishment of exclusive Shiite or Sunni (or Kurdish) neighborhoods—or towns and cities and provinces? We aren't alarmed by the existence of various ethnic quarters in Singapore or, for that matter, Brooklyn, and we accept that Saudi Arabia would not welcome an influx of Christian settlers to Riyadh. What if the last chance for Iraq to survive as a unified state is for its citizens to live in religiously or ethnically separate communities? What if efforts to prevent ethnic cleansing in Baghdad, for example, not only are doomed to fail, but exacerbate the ultimate intensity of the violence? Would we really prefer that a family die in its home, rather than be driven from it? Our principles are noble, but it's shabby to expect Iraqis to die for them.

There are no easy answers to these questions. But it should be absolutely clear by now that ethnic cleansing is an issue we will face again and again in the decades ahead, and it may not always be possible or even helpful to stop its march. We must face the unsettling question as to whether it's always desirable to force a halt to such purges, instead of acting to ameliorate the suffering of those displaced.

Idealists will continue to insist that Arabs and Jews, Sunnis and Shiites, Kurds and Turks, Tajiks and Pashtuns, Sudanese blacks and Arabs, or Nigerian Muslims and Christians can all get along. Would that it were so. But to decline to study the possibility that they might refuse to get along, that the individuals we think we know may be consumed by mass passions that reasonable arguments won't tame, is folly. The old military maxim applies: You may hope for the best, but you prepare for the worst.

There is nothing welcome about ethnic or religious cleansing. But if we do not recognize its insistent reemergence in human affairs, and the fact that—in contrast to full-scale genocide—it remains the lesser evil, we will continue to act ineffectually as the innocent suffer.

Redefining Ethnic Conflict

Charles King

Charles King questions the core differences between those ethnic conflicts that rage for centuries and those that develop peaceful resolutions. He uses Scotland as an example of a nation that has been peaceful for more than two hundred years, while Chechnya, which shares some similarities, has had a history of violence that continues into the twenty-first century. According to King, most civil wars begin because "the basic institutions of security, good government, and social stability have broken down." The differences in the stability of these countries can be traced to the basic foundations of their governments. Charles King is chairman of the faculty of the School of Foreign Service at Georgetown University, where he holds the Ion Ratiu Chair of Romanian Studies. He is the author of The Black Sea: A History.

Every autumn in local parks throughout the United States, thousands of Scots come together to have an ethnic conflict. Kilted chieftains from all the major clans—the MacGregors and Campbells, the McDonalds and Wallaces—march along with tartan banners held high. Bagpipers parade back and forth, drones erect and chanters skirling. Clansmen and clanswomen let out war whoops as they descend onto the soccer field or baseball diamond. Occasionally, someone denounces the English. Eventually, one of the clans receives a trophy for being the fiercest, and then everyone decamps to the beer tent.

These are the peculiar rituals of Scottish Highland games, a large and growing form of weekend entertainment for people of Celtic heritage. But the eager participants, standing in line for a sample of Scotch whisky or a lunch of meat pie and

Charles King, "Scots to Chechens," *Harvard International Review*, vol. 28, Winter 2007, pp. 68–72.

shortbread, are centuries away from a time when the Scots were less quaint: when thousands of people were killed in inter-clan feuding, when Highlanders staged bloody rebellions against English rule, and when the English crown and feudal lords responded with what would now be considered ethnic cleansing—forcibly removing Highland farmers in a sweeping campaign known as the Clearances.

That was the eighteenth century, when northern Scotland was a land of social conflict, violence, and danger. "Till the Highlanders lost their ferocity, with their arms, they suffered from each other all that malignity could dictate, or precipitance could act. . . . Every provocation was revenged with blood, and no man that ventured into a numerous company . . . was sure of returning without a wound," wrote Samuel Johnson during a tour of the region in 1773. His depiction stands in stark contrast to the conditions in modern Scotland, which has been devoid of mobilized violence since the eighteenth century.

But the Scottish example raises an intriguing question: why do some disputes that we now label "ethnic conflicts" seem to endure across the centuries, while others become the purview of suburbanites who happen to spend their weekends puffing on bagpipes? Judging from the Scottish experience, it does not seem unreasonable to believe that being a Chechen, Serb, or Hutu could one day become the same thing as being a Highland Scot. But even posing the question in this way raises important issues about the nature of civil wars and the "ethnic" component of ethnic conflicts.

The Nature of Civil Wars

The 1990s seemed to be the age of ethnic conflict. Around the world, the end of superpower competition heralded a sudden upsurge in age-old animosities. Federations collapsed and genocidal wars broke out, each one over basic differences of religion, language, and history. This is one common reading of the last two decades, but it is in large measure inaccurate.

In the first place, the very label "ethnic conflict" is largely a product of perception and representation, not an analytical tag that describes a unique kind of social violence. No violent conflict ever involves all, or even most, members of one ethnic group suddenly rising up and deciding to kill all the members of another group. This is the cartoon version of ethnic war, but it is seriously out of step with reality.

Rather than an entire ethnic group universally declaring war on another, it is generally small factions of committed militants that execute wars. Governments can also adopt the causes of ethnic, religious, clan, or regional factions, casting themselves as either defenders or avengers of a certain group. However, their determination and brutality can often create the social dividing lines that they claim to be defending. This, in turn, leads to new injustices, which the next generation may seek to avenge.

Mobilized ethnic groups certainly can and do have an effect on politics, but the opposite can also be true: politics can help create mobilized ethnicity in the first place. In other words, "ethnic conflict" is not a meaningful category of analysis until we untangle what we, and the belligerents themselves, really mean by the label.

The second reason to be skeptical about the applicability of the term "ethnic conflict" is that, over the past half century, the great peak in substate violence came not in the 1990s but in the 1960s, during the end of European colonialism. Many of the conflicts that accompanied the end of the British, French, and Portuguese presences in Africa might just as well be labeled "ethnic conflicts" as "postcolonial wars." Indeed, these armed engagements involved battles between groups mobilized along lines of culture and language. Yet because of the analytical lenses in vogue at the time, as well as the public relations strategies of belligerents, these conflicts were usually given political glosses as national liberation struggles or as anti-imperialist revolutions. Superpowers were then easily able to take sides, either supporting or covertly working against their proxies on the ground. The Cold War, in the end, largely determined the labels that analysts applied to substate wars.

Third, most of the 1990s actually saw a decrease in internal armed conflicts, not an escalation. The end of the Cold War proved to be a remarkably positive event in many parts of the world, simply because the United States and the Soviet Union ceased providing overt and covert support to warring parties. Only in Europe and Eurasia did the number of armed conflicts increase, but even there warfare waned as the decade progressed. For many regions, the allegedly chaotic post-Cold War era has been remarkably peaceful in comparison to past decades.

Finally, a great normative change has taken place in the international community in the last half century, and it came fully into force in the 1990s: the preference for negotiated settlements over outright victory. Historically, civil wars have ended in victory, but that outcome has rarely been wrapped in magnanimity. Victors have generally either killed or expelled civilian populations loyal to the losing side, which is, in a way, what happened in the case of Britain's oppression of the Scots during the Highland Clearances more than two centuries ago. Today, however, there is a wide array of international institutions committed to peaceful settlements and a normative legal structure that privileges negotiations over battlefield victory.

Scots, Chechens, and the Myths of Ethnic War

In understanding all of these themes, it is helpful to consider Scotland and Chechnya. Both were distinct regions of larger empires. Both have been divided for centuries between low-landers and highlanders, each with different traditions, economies, and ways of life. Both were religiously distinct from the imperial center and have had long histories of rebellion against imperial rule. In addition, both have been the targets of what we would now call anti-insurgent campaigns, Scotland in the late eighteenth century and Chechnya in the mid-nineteenth century and afterwards. Both produced nations-in-exile, with Scotland sending people to Appalachia, Australia, and other parts of the world throughout the eighteenth and nineteenth centuries, and Chechens being sent to Central Asia in the 1940s. Both peoples, in other words, have a great deal of justifiable animosity towards their imperial oppressors and a history of acting on this anger in a violent manner.

The puzzle, then, is that Scotland and Chechnya ended up so differently—the former as a peaceful European region, the latter as the site of a brutal, decade-long guerrilla war. Perhaps the most important distinction between these two examples is that Scotland has not seen significant violence for more than two centuries. Chechnya, on the other hand, experienced major disruptions during World War I, the Stalinist purges, and World War II, in which Stalin ordered the entire Chechen population deported for alleged collaboration with the Nazis. Chechnya is, thus, one of the best examples of the fact that violence in the recent past increases the risk of violence in the present.

The Peril of Misplaced Historicism

These examples also illustrate that there are deeper issues concerning the meaning of the term "ethnic conflict." In fact, the mere question of why some countries, regions, or peoples have turned out to be more violent than others illustrates three basic problems at the heart of how we think about ethnicity, identity, and war.

First is the peril of misplaced historicism. When the leaders of belligerent groups claim that some long-forgotten battle or ancient wrong is the impetus for their struggle, it is tempting to take them at their word. . . .

A Scottish bagpipe band proudly marches through a field in unison. Scotland is an example of a country that has been able to resolve conflict and war, which in effect has brought peace to the nation for more than two hundred years. © Pictorial Press Ltd/Alamy.

However, interpreting the present by referring to the misty past is mainly a matter of propaganda. In many intergroup disputes, there is no linear connection between distant forms of social mobilization and those that take place today. They are as disconnected as a suburban "Scotsman" is from a Highland shepherd of yore. Drawing lines from the past to the present is a purely political act, not an analytical one.

History does not make violence either inevitable or more likely. The reason is simple: there are far more bad historians in the world than there are leaders of ethnic armies. There simply were no Scots in the eighteenth century, at least not in the sense of a unified ethnic group with clear and common interests. Instead, there were highlanders and lowlanders, feudal lords and farmers, urban merchants and itinerant intellectuals. There were likewise no Serbs, Tutsis, Albanians, or Chechens, at least not with the meanings that those labels have come to hold hundreds of years later. In interpreting the past, it is important to avoid applying such ethnic labels to individuals who may have had no real conception of themselves as belonging to such a group.

Moreover, not every instance in which some group feels aggrieved for the injustices inflicted upon their alleged ancestors produces an ethnic conflict. . . . History is important mainly to the extent that leaders manipulate it to their own benefit. It is not a record of grievances that will inevitably turn violent of their own accord.

This is not to say that history plays no role in determining intergroup violence. However, it is usually the more immediate history of interethnic relations that is critical—the history that has been recently experienced and can be remembered by the current generation of political leaders and their constituents. In the former Yugoslavia, memories of interethnic violence during World War II turned out to be important sources of grass-roots mobilization. As the chaos of war spread from neighborhood to neighborhood, citizens could remember what a neighbor's grandfather had done to their own relatives during the previous war. Some of these individuals were not above using the circumstances of social breakdown to exact personal revenge.

Recent institutions matter as well. In Rwanda, Russia, and elsewhere, social categories created by previous governments—from the colonial era, for example, or during the Soviet period—became lines along which groups were mobilized. It is these kinds of personal memories and social institutions that are the real catalysts of intergroup violence, not the imagined grievances of long-ago eras.

Uncritical "Groupism"

A second problem with the term "ethnic conflict" is what might be called uncritical "groupism," an issue which Rogers Brubaker explores in detail in his brilliant collection of essays,

Ethnicity Without Groups. As Brubaker argues, both nationalists and analysts of ethno-national conflict see the world as a collection of groups—masses of distinct colors spreading across the cartographical landscape. Reality is, of course, more complicated. Not all those whom we might label "Chechen" or "Hutu" think of themselves in terms of such categories. And even if they do, these labels compete with many other forms of identity, such as social class, religion, or regional affiliation.

Humans have a wide array of identities with which they associate at various times. The aim of the ethnic entrepreneur or the purveyor of violent mobilization is to convince significant numbers of people to select only one of those identities, the ethnic one, and subordinate all the others to it. Thus, when analysts interpret "ethnic conflicts" only in terms of the alleged groups involved, they play immediately into the hands of those who have "ethnicized" the conflict in the first place—casting it as a war between entire groups, rather than between mobilized individuals claiming to act on those groups' behalf.

Such terminology applies the metaphor of interstate war to a much more irregular and complicated form of violence. When we say that Germany invaded Poland in 1939, we mean that the regular army of the German state crossed an internationally recognized boundary and used military force illegitimately against its neighbor. But when we say that "the Serbs" attacked towns and villages in eastern Bosnia in 1995, we are saying something far less clear. It was, of course, not the case that all ethnic Serbs in the former Yugoslavia made war on all Bosnian Muslims, nor that those who were fighting in "Serb" units were all ethnic Serbs. It is small groups of violent entrepreneurs, not entire populations, that create the conditions for large-scale violence. Yet by taking ethnic leaders at their word and recognizing a small set of violent entrepreneurs as spokesmen for a larger population, analysts often become party to the conflict itself.

The Danger of Poor Governance

Beyond historicism and groupism, there is yet another key component to the way in which we understand ethnicized disputes, and it has to do with the issue of governance. Most civil wars begin because the basic institutions of security, good governance, and social stability have broken down. Large-scale ethnic mobilization usually takes place when the bounds of ethnic membership become politically salient. People rely on ethnic leaders for protection. They turn toward ethnic confreres for security. In an environment of uncertainty and lawlessness, they come to see ethnicity as a shorthand way of telling friend from foe. Mobilized ethnicity, in other words, is generally a product, not a cause, of state breakdown. . . .

Dealing with "Ethnicized" Disputes

None of these arguments concerning the nature of ethnicity and conflict can gainsay the problem of dealing with violent disputes once they have become ethnicized. Once people are systematically targeted because of their ethnicity, race, religion, or regional affiliation, it is difficult to claim that a conflict has not become a genuinely ethnic one. Once groups come to see themselves as uniquely victimized or privileged because of their ethnicity, talk of inaccurate history, misplaced groupism, or dysfunctional governments seems beside the point.

But this is an overly narrow view of the issue. Even in the depths of the bloodiest and most intractable conflicts—from Bosnia to Darfur, and from Chechnya to sectarian Iraq—there is still space for non-ethnic solutions. The international community's tack has normally been to look for the least costly way out. This method usually involves buying off violent entrepreneurs by rewarding their communal groups, redrawing boundary lines, crafting new communal institutions, and cementing the very social divisions that the militants worked hard to establish.

This kind of solution may be an inevitable part of international politics, given the prevailing opinion regarding ethnic conflict. If countries are insufficiently committed to recasting the basic terms of ethnic violence, there may be no choice but to accede to the versions of history and identity that those with the most weapons in hand preach and defend. Such solutions are not flawed because they are ineffective in ending ethnic conflict, although this may, in fact, be true. They are flawed because they are founded upon reasoning and terminology that are formulated as propaganda devices rather than analytical tools.

Within any conflict, there are always multiple interpretations of the basic issues at stake: the boundary lines between friend and foe, the fundamental causes of the dispute, and the design of a reasonable solution. The challenge for peacemakers is to identify and embolden those voices that seek to recast the terms of the debate, rather than those that attribute the violence to age-old and irreconcilable social divisions. Negotiations must focus on the true nature of the conflict and avoid rhetoric and reasoning that adopts ethnic terminology and explanations. More often than not, the ethnic divisions upon which the conflict in question is based are a product of violence and not its original cause.

So, in light of this argument, can Chechens ever become Scots? There is no reason to expect that they cannot—although it would take a massive immigration of ethnic Chechens to the United States, Canada, and Australia to replicate the Scottish experience. The point is that misreading history, groupism, and governance can lead analysts to amplify, rather than interpret, the claims that nationalists, ethnic cleansers, and violent entrepreneurs tend to make. Critiquing the labels we use ought to be the starting point for real analysis. Otherwise, we will be left with the difficult task of having to explain why one history of violence, ethnic cleansing, and exile produced a long cycle of death and retribution, while another simply produced suburban men in skirts.

Culture, Not Race, Will Determine If Democracy Will Succeed

Lawrence E. Harrison

Lawrence E. Harrison is the director of the Cultural Change Institute at the Fletcher School at Tufts University. The author of numerous works including Underdevelopment Is a State of Mind: The Latin American Case *and* Who Prospers: How Cultural Values Shape Economic and Political Success *and coeditor with Samuel Huntington of* Culture Matters: How Values Shape Human Progress, *Harrison directed U.S. Agency for International Development missions in several Latin American countries between 1965 and 1981.*

In the following selection, Harrison contends that multiculturalism, which he defines as "the idea that all cultures are essentially equal," is a failed political concept. His thesis is that culture matters—that there are certain values, beliefs, and traditions inherent in some cultures that promote the growth of democracy and social justice, while other cultures have values uncongenial to the principles of democratic governance. He urges that culture be considered in the development of foreign policy, recommending that cultural transformation needs to take place before democratic progress can be made. Instead of multiculturalism, he urges that the United States and Canada promote acculturation to the Anglo-Protestant cultural mainstream, whose virtues he maintains have led to progress.

Future generations may look back on Iraq and immigration as the two great disasters of the [George W.] Bush presi-

Lawrence E. Harrison, "The End of Multiculturalism," The *National Interest*, vol. 93, January-February 2008, pp. 88–96.

dency. Ironically, for a conservative administration, both of these policy initiatives were rooted in a multicultural view of the world.

Since the 1960s, multiculturalism, the idea that all cultures are essentially equal, has become a dominant feature of the political and intellectual landscape of the West. It has profoundly influenced Iraq War policy, the policy of democracy promotion, international development agendas and immigration policy, with consequences for the cultural composition of societies.

But multiculturalism rests on a frail foundation: Cultural relativism, the notion that no culture is better or worse than any other—it is merely different. That's doubtlessly good advice for cultural anthropologists doing ethnographic studies in the field. If one's goal is full understanding of a value system quite different from one's own, ethnocentrism can seriously distort the quest and the conclusions. But what if the objective is to assess the extent to which a culture nurtures values, attitudes and beliefs that facilitate progress toward democratic governance, social justice and an end to poverty, the goals of the UN Universal Declaration of Human Rights? The idea that some cultures are more nurturing than others of progress thus defined—and that this assumption can be measured and assessed—challenges the very essence of cultural relativism.

The idea also has major implications for a variety of domestic and foreign policies, from the ability of a country to absorb large numbers of new immigrants to the ease with which one expects to export democracy and free-market systems. Why, for example, have free-market economic reforms worked well in India yet poorly in Latin America (Chile excepted), where socialism, even authoritarian socialism in the case of [Venezuelan president] Hugo Chavez's Venezuela, appears to be alive and well?

Cultural factors do not wholly explain political, economic, and social success or failure, but surely they are relevant—as more than two decades of research . . . has demonstrated. Yet many policymakers are uncomfortable addressing cultural differences, even when there is clear evidence that culture matters.

Multiculturalism and Foreign Policy

If culture matters, then, by influencing the degree of receptivity of a society to democracy and free-market institutions and the degree to which the society is just and produces and encourages entrepreneurs, what are the implications for a foreign policy, a fundament of which is the doctrine that "These values of freedom are right and true for every person, in every society"?—this implies that any culture in the world is capable of sustaining a functioning democracy. The Bush Administration has staked huge human, financial, diplomatic and prestige resources on the doctrine's applicability in Iraq. It is now apparent that the doctrine is fallacious.

What were the chances of consolidating democracy—not just elections, but also the full array of political rights and civil liberties—in Iraq, an Arab country with no real experience with democracy and with two conflict-prone Islamic sects, Sunni and Shi'a, and an ethnolinguistic group, the Kurds, seeking autonomy? And why did people think that this would ignite a "democracy wave" that would sweep through the region, when many of the preconditions associated with a successful transition to democracy—including societal openness and literacy, particularly female literacy—were lacking?. . .

The Arab world is not fertile soil for the rapid cultivation of democracy.

A key component of a successful democratic transition is trust. Trust is a particularly important cultural factor for social justice and prosperity. Trust in others reduces the cost of economic transactions, and democratic stability depends on it.

Trust is periodically measured in some eighty countries by the World Values Survey. Four Nordic countries—Denmark,

Sweden, Norway and Finland—enjoy very high levels of trust: 58–67 percent of respondents in these countries believe that most people can be trusted. By contrast, 12 percent of respondents in Zimbabwe and South Africa, 11 percent in Algeria, 8 percent in Tanzania and Uganda, and 3 percent of Brazilians believe that most people can be trusted. There are no survey data for Iraq, but the data from the other Middle Eastern states are not particularly encouraging.

The high levels of identification and trust in Nordic societies reflect their homogeneity; common Lutheran antecedents, including a rigorous ethical code and heavy emphasis on education; and a consequent sense of the nation as one big family imbued with the Golden Rule. In sharp contrast, Cameroon's Daniel Etounga-Manguelle [head of a consulting company operating in Africa] points to some of the cultural factors that help explain the low levels of trust in Africa and the propensity of the region for corruption and strife: fatalism, authoritarianism and a communitarianism that suffocates both individual initiative and economic rationality. One can point to many of the same factors in Iraq—to which the current ethno-sectarian conflicts vividly attest.

If nothing else, the Iraq adventure demonstrates the enormous risks that attend a foreign policy predicated on President Bush's view, expressed when he met Indonesian President [Susilo Barnbang] Yudhyono in November 2006, that "freedom is universal and democracy is universal." But it also underscores the need to appreciate the role culture plays in all aspects of foreign affairs—and the cultural competence necessary in all foreign-affairs agencies, including the Department of Defense.

Multiculturalism and International Development

Another area where the sway of multiculturalism is apparent is international development. Development of poor countries in all its dimensions—political, social and economic—has been a priority goal of the advanced democracies, motivated by both pragmatic (e.g., reduced international strife, increased trade, reduced illegal immigration) and humanitarian motives.

But most development-assistance institutions have thus far failed to address cultural obstacles to progress and the need for cultural change. Their avoidance of culture is in part attributable to culture-blind economists—and anthropologists and other social scientists committed to cultural relativism—who have dominated policy. The four UN Development Program Arab Human Development Reports are courageous exceptions.

Cultural relativism fits very nicely with, and reinforces, the predilection of many economists to assume "that people are the same everywhere and will respond to the right economic opportunities and incentives"—a point made by former World Bank economist William Easterly when he reviewed my book *Who Prospers?* How, then, would Easterly explain why, in multicultural countries where the economic opportunities and incentives are available to all, some ethnic or religious minorities do much better than majority populations. This has been true, for example, of any place the Chinese have migrated, from Indonesia, Malaysia, the Philippines and Thailand—all the way to the United States and Canada.

Or what about differences that emerge between countries in the same region of the world, with similar geographical attributes and populations of the same general ethnic stock? Haiti is the poorest, least literate, most misgoverned, most corrupt country in the Western Hemisphere, substantial aid from the United States, Canada, the World Bank, and other bilateral and multilateral donors notwithstanding. The dominant belief system, Voodoo, is based on sorcery. Hundreds of spirits, very human and capricious, control human destinies. The only way to gain leverage over what happens in one's life is to propitiate them through the ceremonial intervention of the Voodoo priests and priestesses. What you do, whether you live your life ethically, is irrelevant to the spirits; what matters only is that they be, in essence, "bribed." Voodoo is thus a major contributor to the high levels of mistrust, paranoia, sense of helplessness and despair noted in the anthropological literature about Haiti.

Voodoo's roots are in the Dahomey region of West Africa, whence came most of the slaves the French imported into "Saint Domingue," Haiti's colonial predecessor. Dahomey is today the country of Benin, where the indicators of income, child malnutrition, child mortality, life expectancy and literacy are strikingly similar to those for Haiti. But we see a far different picture when we examine Barbados, another Caribbean island that, like Haiti, was populated largely by slaves from Dahomey. Barbados was shaped by British values and institutions—it was a British colony until 1966; Haiti won its independence from France in 1804. Barbadians are sometimes referred to as "Afro-Saxons" or "Black Englishmen." Barbados is a prosperous democracy, number thirty on the 2005 UN Human Development Index, ahead of the Czech Republic, Argentina, Poland and Chile. It is approaching First World status.

These divergent outcomes are not accidents. Culture does matter. Race doesn't. . . .

The considerable intelligence, creativity and dedication of development professionals over the past half-century have not succeeded in transforming the large majority of poor, unjust, authoritarian societies. Where transformations have occurred, they usually either have been nurtured by cultures that contain progress-prone elements (e.g., the Confucian societies of east Asia) or have been cases where cultural change has been central to the transformation (e.g., Spain, Ireland or Quebec).

I want to stress that the Culture Matters paradigm does not present democracy and progress as being the exclusive preserve of particular nations. Even the West had to undergo a period of cultural transformation to discard the progress-resistant elements in its own culture. That transformation is still far from complete in some parts of "the West."

The Iraq adventure has powerfully reinforced the lesson that cultural change must be led from within a society. A critical mass of native political, intellectual and religious leaders who recognize that some aspects of the traditional culture present obstacles to popular aspirations for a better life is indispensable. Efforts to encourage change from the outside are likely to be resented, resisted and labeled "cultural imperialism."

Cultural change is not easy, and the culture paradigm is not a magic wand. But adding cultural change to the array of other development-assistance tools should, in the long run, significantly accelerate the rate of progress in those countries that choose to take the paradigm seriously.

A Matter of Migration

We often see these issues as only affecting other countries and only U.S. interests overseas. But what happens when we ponder the domestic implications? One issue largely overlooked in recent debates over immigration is the impact when an unprecedented number of people from "low-trust" cultures immigrate to the United States.

In 1990, 52 percent of Americans and a like percentage of Canadians believed that most people could be trusted. In 2000, the proportion of trusting Americans had dropped to 36 percent; of trusting Canadians, to 39 percent.

While there are doubtlessly many factors contributing to this troubling slide, multiculturalism may well be one of them. This is apparent in two senses: First, immigrants from areas like Africa and Latin America bring their native cultures' mistrust with them, and, second, the presence of significant numbers of "strangers"—people who may speak a foreign language, dress differently, behave differently—may leave people in the mainstream doubtful of their trustworthiness. Both undermine [what writer Roger Doyle has described as] "social capital"—"a high level of trust and tolerance, an egalitarian spirit, volunteerism, an interest in keeping informed, and participation in public affairs." . . .

In *The Americano Dream*, Mexican-American Lionel Sosa argues that the value system that has retarded progress in Latin America is an impediment to the upward mobility of Latin American immigrants in the United States. So does former U.S. Congressman Herman Badillo, a Puerto Rican whose book *One Nation, One Standard* is both an indictment of Latino undervaluing of education and a call for cultural change.

The progress of Hispanic immigrants, not to mention harmony in the broader society, depends, then, on their acculturation to the values of that broader society. Efforts—for example, long-term bilingual education—to perpetuate "old country" values in a multicultural salad bowl undermine acculturation to the mainstream—and upward mobility—and are likely to result in continuing under-achievement, poverty, resentment and divisiveness. So too does the willy-nilly emergence of bilingualism in the United States—no language in our history has ever before competed with English to the point where one daily hears commercial enterprises responding to telephone calls with, "If you want to speak in English, press one; Si quiere hablar en espanol, oprima el boton numero dos [if you speak Spanish, press number two]."

Because language is the conduit of culture, the perpetuation of Spanish as a second national language of the United States implies the perpetuation of Latino culture. There is no word for "compromise" in Spanish, nor is there a Spanish word that captures the full meaning of the English word "dissent." A prominent Nicaraguan educator with a Harvard Ph.D. once told me that for Latin Americans, "dissent" (disenso, disension) is close to "heresy"—something that has been noted with respect to other languages, such as Russian. Moreover, as the Costa Rican psychiatrist Luis Diego Herrera points out in his essay in *Developing Cultures: Essays on Cultural Change*, many Spanish verb forms are passive reflexive (e.g., "It fell" rather than "I dropped it." "It got broken" rather than "I broke it."), a verbal structure that may nurture a lack of a sense of accountability.

Immigration Success Stories

But while there is much to be concerned about with respect to immigrants from Mexico, and Latin America more generally, this is not true of all immigrants. The experience of immigrants from China, Korea and Japan contrasts strikingly with that of Latino immigrants. The Asians' rapid upward mobility is evidenced by their vastly disproportionate numbers at our most prestigious universities. Making up about 5 percent of the U.S. population, Asians constitute 41 percent of undergraduates at the University of California at Berkeley, 27 percent at MIT, 24 percent at Stanford and 18 percent at Harvard. The success of Asian-Americans reminds us of the east Asian "miracles"—initially economic, but now also, in several cases, political. East Asian immigrants have found it easier to adapt in part because they are influenced by traditional Confucian culture, which, like Jewish culture (Jews may be even more disproportionately represented in elite universities), shares some central values with America's dominant Anglo-Protestant culture. Both cultures emphasize "progress-prone" values, such as education, the belief that a person can influence his destiny, wealth is the product of individual creativity and advancement should be based on merit.

Among other elements of U.S. Anglo-Protestant culture relevant to success are the rule of law; fair play; individual rights; limits on governmental authority; a blend of individualism and sense of community; freedom, including freedom of religion; and an ethical code that breeds trust. These values are substantially shared by other countries of the Euro-Atlantic and east Asian communities; but this is emphatically not so in the case of the Islamic world, Africa and Latin America.

Framing the Immigration Debate

So far, the immigration debate in the United States has been framed largely in economic terms (although border security and environmental concerns are also clearly in play)—producing some odd pro-immigration bedfellows, such as the editorial pages of *The New York Times* and *The Wall Street Journal.* Most policymakers have sparred over the questions of whether the U.S. economy needs more unskilled immigrants, whether immigrants take jobs away from U.S. citizens, to what extent immigrants are responsible for draining resources (e.g., with respect to education and health expenses), and whether or not population growth, importantly driven by immigration, is necessary for a healthy economy.

But immigration looks very different when viewed in cultural terms, particularly with respect to the vast legal and illegal Latino immigration, as many as a million or more people a year, most of them with few skills and little education. To be sure, the United States has absorbed large numbers of unskilled and uneducated immigrants in the past, and today the large majority of their descendants are in the cultural mainstream. But the numbers of Latino immigrants and their geographic concentration today leave real doubts about the prospects for acculturation: 70 percent of children in the Los Angeles public schools and 60 percent in the Denver schools are Latino.

Policy Implications

So culture needs to be added to the debate on a variety of foreign and domestic policies. It may be too late for Iraq, but migration and development are ongoing issues. And if multiculturalism is a myth, how do we avoid the woes that will inevitably attend the creation of an enduring and vast underclass alienated from the upwardly mobile cultural mainstream? Some policy implications, one for Latin America, the others for the United States and Canada, are apparent.

First, Latin American political, intellectual, religious and other leaders should heed the advice of prominent writers like Osvaldo Hurtado and journalists Mariano Grondona and Carlos Alberto Montaner. They must reject the "foreign devils" explanations for Latin America's development shortcomings, for example, "dependency" and anti-capitalist neo-liberalismo. They must instead focus inward on those features of traditional Latin American culture that are obstacles to the consolidation of democracy, social justice and prosperity, among them authoritarianism, elitism, fatalism, absence of long-term focus, a low priority for education, and an emphasis on connections and amiguismo rather than merit. And here, the transformations undergone by Spain and Portugal that have vaulted both into the Western European democratic-capitalist mainstream provide a culturally relevant model for the rest of Latin America—as opposed to regressing toward failed socialist/authoritarian "solutions" of the Hugo Chavez variety.

Second, the flow of immigrants into the United States must be calibrated not only to the needs of the economy—and it bears remembering that new arrivals have particularly affected in negative ways low-income American citizens, disproportionately African-American and Hispanic, as Barbara Jordan [former member of the U.S. House of Representatives from Texas] stressed as chair of the 1990s Immigration Reform Commission—but also to the capacity of the United States to assure acculturation of the immigrants. We must be a melting pot, not a salad bowl. The melting pot, the essence of which is our Anglo-Protestant cultural tradition, is our way of creating the homogeneity that has contributed so much to the trust and mutual identification—and progress—of the Nordic societies.

Finally, as with the immigration flows of the late 19th and early twentieth centuries, an extensive program of activities designed to facilitate acculturation, including mastery of English, should be mounted. A law declaring English to be the national language is one measure that would be helpful in this respect. And tasking respected social scientists with periodic assessments of acculturation of the burgeoning Hispanic minority would also provide useful benchmarks.

The costs of multiculturalism—in terms of disunity, the clash of classes and declining trust—are likely to be huge in the long run. All cultures are not equal when it comes to promoting progress, and very few can match Anglo-Protestantism in this respect. The United States and Canada should be promoting acculturation to the national mainstream, not a mythical, utopian multiculturalism. And they should take care that the Anglo-Protestant virtues that have brought them so far do not fall into disrepair, let alone disrepute.

For Further Discussion

1. Sean Smith writes that J.K. Rowling is proudest of the chapter "The Mirror of Erised," of which she says, "When I reread the chapter I saw that I had given Harry lots of my own feelings about my own mother's death." Harry says that his mother, who was born to Muggle parents, "died to save me." What importance does Harry's mother have to the theme of ethnic purity in the series?
2. Dana Goldstein, Giselle Liza Anatol, Rachel Dempsey, and Andrew Blake contend that, although the world of Harry Potter seems multicultural and the ethnic cleansing practiced by Lord Voldemort is denounced, there are racial and gender stereotypes in the series. These authors point to the obvious superiority of wizards over Muggles as one example of this. Do you agree with this interpretation? Why or why not?
3. Julia Turner, Judith Rauhofer, and Nathaniel Rivers write that, after the terrorist attacks of September 11, 2001, the Harry Potter series became increasingly darker as Rowling incorporated into her plots events from the war on terror. Do you agree with Judith Rauhofer that Rowling is criticizing the U.K. and U.S. governments' response to terrorism? Do you agree with Julia Turner that Rowling is using terrorism as a way of instilling fear in her readers? A major theme of the Harry Potter books is the battle between good and evil. How is terrorism relevant to this theme?
4. In his essay in Chapter 3, Lawrence E. Harrison takes issue with political multiculturalism. He makes a distinction between culture and race, arguing that certain cultures are steeped in traditions that provide a frail foundation for

democracy and stable governments. Do you agree with his thesis? Cite nationalities or cultures not mentioned in his article to support your position.

5. In Chapter 3 Ralph Peters writes that while ethnic cleansing is insupportable, some forms of it, namely ethnic separation, are preferable if the alternative is full-scale genocide. What are the differences between ethnic cleansing and genocide? Can you think of some examples in history where ethnic cleansing may have been preferable to genocide?

For Further Reading

Lloyd Alexander, *The Prydain Chronicles*. 5 vols. New York: Holt, Rinehart and Winston, 1964–1968.

Susan Cooper, *The Dark Is Rising*. 5 vols. New York: Simon Pulse, 2007. Originally published 1965–1977.

Joseph Delaney, The Last Apprentice Series. 5 vols. Greenwillow Books, 2004–2008.

Jessica Day George, *Dragon Slippers*. New York: Bloomsbury Children's Books, 2007.

Ursula K. Le Guin, *The Earthsea Trilogy*. London: Penguin, 1979.

Ursula K. Le Guin, *Tehanu: The Last Book of Earthsea*. New York: Atheneum, 1990.

C.S. Lewis, *The Complete Chronicles of Narnia*. New York: HarperCollins, 1998. Originally published 1950–1956.

Christopher Paolini, The Inheritance Cycle. New York: Alfred A. Knopf, 2003–.

Rick Riordan, Percy Jackson and the Olympians series. New York: Miramax Books/Hyperion Books for Children, 2005–.

J.R.R. Tolkien, *The Lord of the Rings*. 3 vols. London: Allen & Unwin, 1954–1955.

Rick Yancey, *The Extraordinary Adventures of Alfred Kropp*. New York, London, Berlin: Bloomsbury, 2005.

Bibliography

Books

David Baggett and Shawn E. Klein, eds.	*Harry Potter and Philosophy: If Aristotle Ran Hogwarts*. Chicago: Open Court, 2004.
George W. Beahm	*Muggles and Magic: J.K. Rowling and the Harry Potter Phenomenon*. Charlottesville, VA: Hampton Roads Publishing Company, 2004.
Andrew Bell-Fialkoff	*Ethnic Cleansing*. New York: St. Martin's Press, 1996.
David Colbert	*The Magical Worlds of Harry Potter: A Treasury of Myths, Legends, and Fascinating Facts*. Wrightsville Beach, NC: Lumina Press, 2001.
Lindsey Fraser	*An Interview with J.K. Rowling*. London: Mammoth, 2000.
Elizabeth E. Heilman, ed.	*Harry Potter's World: Multidisciplinary Critical Perspectives*. New York: RoutledgeFalmer, 2003.
Connie Ann Kirk	*J.K. Rowling: A Biography*. Westport, CT: Greenwood Press, 2003.
Allan Zola Kronzek and Elizabeth Kronzek	*The Sorcerer's Companion: A Guide to the Magical World of Harry Potter*. New York: Broadway Books, 2001.

Will Kymlicka	*Multicultural Odysseys: Navigating the New International Politics of Diversity.* New York: Oxford University Press, 2007.
Philip Nel	*J.K. Rowling's Harry Potter Novels: A Reader's Guide.* New York: Continuum, 2001.
Anne Phillips	*Multiculturalism Without Culture.* Princeton, NJ: Princeton University Press, 2007.
Lana A. Whited, ed.	*The Ivory Tower and Harry Potter: Perspectives on a Literary Phenomenon.* Columbia, MO: University of Missouri Press, 2002.

Articles

Brycchan Carey	"Hermione and the House-Elves: The Literary and Historical Contexts of J.K. Rowling's Antislavery Campaign." In *Reading Harry Potter: Critical Essays,* edited by Giselle Liza Anatol. Westport, CT: Praeger, 2003.
Nancy Gibbs	"Person of the Year Runner-Up: #3 J.K. Rowling," *Time,* December 31, 2007.
Paul Hoffman	"Human Rights and Terrorism," *Human Rights Quarterly* 26, no. 4 (November 2004): 932–955.

David Long	"Quidditch, Imperialism, and the Sport-War Intertext." In *Harry Potter and International Relations*, edited by Daniel H. Nexon and Iver B. Neumann. Lanham, MD: Rowman & Littlefield, 2006.
Michele Marchand	"A Wizard's Guide to Fighting Terrorism," *Real Change*, July 24, 2003. www.realchangenews.org/2003/2003_07_24/features/a_wizards_guide.html.
Patrick Morgan	"The Dangers of Ethnic Nationalism," *Quadrant Magazine* 52, no. 6 (June 2008).
Iver B. Neumann	"Naturalizing Geography: Harry Potter and the Realms of Muggles, Magic Folks, and Giants." In *Harry Potter and International Relations*, edited by Daniel H. Nexon and Iver B. Neumann. Lanham, MD: Rowman & Littlefield, 2006.
Judy O'Malley	"Talking with . . . J.K. Rowling," *Book Links*, July 1999.
Elaine Ostry	"Accepting Mudbloods: The Ambivalent Social Vision of J.K. Rowling's Fairy Tales." In *Reading Harry Potter: Critical Essays*, edited by Giselle Liza Anatol. Westport, CT: Praeger, 2003.

Julia Park	"Class and Socioeconomic Identity in Harry Potter's England." In *Reading Harry Potter: Critical Essays*, edited by Giselle Liza Anatol. Westport, CT: Praeger, 2003.
Andrea Sachs	"*The Dark Side: The Inside Story of How the War on Terror Turned into a War on American Ideals*, by Jane Mayer." *Time*, July 28, 2008.
Wendy Smith	"The Abuses of Enchantment: Why Some Children's Classics Give Parents the Creeps." *American Scholar* 74, no. 4 (Autumn 2005).
Catherine Viglienzoni	"No Politics in Harry Potter," *Berkeley Beacon*, November 1, 2007. www.berkeleybeacon.com.

Index

C

D

H

M

N

S

W

X